## DEDICATION

This book is dedicated to those men and women who allowed me, a complete stranger, to probe deeply into their lives and their minds. Without their cooperation, this book could not have been written.

iv

# ACKNOWLEDGMENTS

A real debt of gratitude is owed to my good friend, critic, and adviser, Lin Fraser, M.A./MFCC. If I had not met her, this book probably would never have been written. Had it not been for her enthusiasm in promoting interviews in the gender community for my research, the project would never have gotten off the ground.

George P. Fulmer, M.D., has been a constant source of information and encouragement. His constructive criticism has been an invaluable resource, and he has always found the time to answer medical questions I have had. Above all, he is a kind and gentle man.

My very dear friend, Renah Shnaider, has furnished the emotional nourishment I needed to keep sifting through issues which sometimes seemed so hopelessly complicated that I questioned my ability to be able to explain them in comprehensible language. She read every chapter of this book as it was finished, and her enthusiasm always provided me with the incentive to continue.

A very special thanks has to go to Kelley Ware, a very special person in my life. She not only has given me encouragement, but provided me with a sounding board. I was able to bounce ideas and concepts off of her, and her responses were always considered, direct, and very honest.

My good friend, Maureen O'Conner, M.S., has not only provided much needed support and encouragement, but as a Speech and Language Pathologist, her professional expertise and her willingness to share it have added a great deal to this book.

Paul Walker, Ph.D., because of his vast knowledge of gender and sexuality which he has generously shared with the public through his writings, presentations, and interviews, has contributed immensely to this book. I have been able to quote him from a number of sources. When I first started this project and requested his help, he asked to meet with me; he questioned me very carefully before he referred people to me for interviews. I owe him special thanks for those many referrals.

Joanna M. Clark, Chairperson of the Transsexual Rights Committee of the Southern California Chapter of the American Civil Liberties Union, was most kind in answering my questions regarding the civil liberties of transsexuals. Her lobbying efforts on behalf of transsexuals have been monumental. Many transsexuals owe her much, although they may not be aware of her relentless pursuit of their interests.

My friend, Jude Paton, M.A., PAC, has been a real inspiration through his support and our exchange of ideas and information. I have to express my admiration for the personal time and energy he has devoted to helping transsexuals.

I offer my thanks to Jack Leibman, M.D., who is with the Department of Public Health, Center For Special Problems, City and County of San Francisco, California, for his interest and for referring persons to me to be interviewed. The involvement and cooperation of professionals like Dr. Leibman have been indispensable in allowing me to gather research material.

The eagle eye of Suzanne L. Daly simply would not allow me to misplace commas and spell creatively, as is sometimes my wont. She deserves much credit for a readable text.

K.E.S.

# TABLE OF CONTENTS

# FOREWORD

As a therapist who works with transsexuals on a daily basis, I have been hoping a good book on the subject would be written by someone. There is very little worthwhile information available on the subject of transsexualism to which I can refer patients, their families and friends, and others interested in the subject. *The Uninvited Dilemma* fulfills my hope. Ms. Stuart has now provided everyone with an accurate, up-to-date, and very understandable picture of the transsexual dilemma.

The author has not depended upon theoreticians, clinical descriptions, or occasional autobiographies which have been the only material available until now. She has gone into the field and developed her insights from talking to transsexuals themselves. Her research is extensive, thorough, and extremely well conceived. Ms. Stuart, in short, has done her homework, and her book reflects it.

*The Uninvited Dilemma* is the most objective examination of transsexualism I have read. The author did not confine her research or her writing to only one aspect of the dilemma. She looks at the whole person, not just individual aspects of behavior. Ms. Stuart digs deep, and she draws a realistic picture of the feelings transsexuals have, how the dilemma affects their lives as children and adults, and how it affects those around them. Her descriptions of relationships transsexuals have with their loved ones is sensitive, yet she eschews passing judgment. When she describes how very young children are likely to react to transsexual parents, one cannot help but be moved by her sensitivity and understanding of the human mind.

Ms. Stuart shows no fear in discussing some very controversial subjects. The issue of sexuality, particularly sexual preference in relationship to transsexualism is met head-on. She also does not hesitate to question the widely held theory of a continuum or gray area between transsexualism and transvestism. One has to admire her very careful reasoning with respect to these very complex issues. One of the things I like best about Ms. Stuart's discussions is that when she gives an opinion, or proposes a theory, she tells us it is opinion or theory; and that is very refreshing.

The substance of *The Uninvited Dilemma* is not theory or speculation, however, and the book supplies badly needed information written in a clear, concise manner. Ms.

Stuart gives the reader a graphic understanding of what gender means and the difference between gender and sexuality. The author introduces two new terms which I feel are very constructive and provide a much better understanding of the transsexual process than less precise terms which have been used in the past. Above all, Ms. Stuart has translated complex biological, medical, and psychological terms and concepts into interesting and very understandable language. The book is based on painstaking research, and my years of clinical experience confirm the validity of this book in almost every respect. Ms. Stuart's conclusions about the subject of transsexualism are completely in accord with my experience as a therapist; she has managed to paint a very vivid picture of transsexualism in a very interesting style.

Not only will *The Uninvited Dilemma* be of great help to transsexuals and their families, but it will do much to dispel the many misconceptions the general public and some transsexuals have about the condition. It also should help transsexuals throw off some of the sense of guilt they have, and be able to confront their dilemmas without the stigma of responsibility so many of them experience. This book should be required reading for all who study gender and human sexuality, and it should find its way into the libraries of all persons in the medical and mental health professions, because it will arm them with current, accurate, and much needed information about a widely misunderstood condition.

Lin Fraser, M.A./MFCC

# PREFACE

This book is about transsexuals. The subject has received widespread publicity; but despite the headlines, little is known about the condition by the general public, and this is true of many transsexuals. Transsexualism is usually thought of as a sexual aberration, though readers will learn it is a gender condition. This is a serious book, and readers looking for salacious material will have to turn elsewhere. This book concerns feelings people experience, for the most part.

A number of years ago, I became friends with a therapist who treats transsexuals as well as persons with gender confusion or sexual conditions. The more we talked, the more I realized how little was known about the subject, and how many misconceptions people have about this condition. I decided to write a book about the subject, not based on what I had read, or what my friend had told me; rather, on a foundation of what transsexuals could tell me about their lives. I wanted to talk to transsexuals and find out how they viewed the condition and what their feelings were. After reading as much as I could find on the subject, I designed an interview to help me achieve my goals. I interviewed seventy–five transsexuals and talked extensively with another twenty–five or thirty of them. I also talked at length with a number of homosexuals and transvestites. Additionally, I talked with and consulted physicians and therapists who have extensive experience dealing with transsexuals.

The book covers a wide range of subjects which are relevant to transsexualism. Various words and terms used in connection with the subject are explained. There is a detailed discussion of gender and sexuality. Various relationships transsexuals have throughout their lives (including family, spouses, and children) are explored, as well as how their conditions affect those relationships. One chapter is devoted to the years transsexuals spent in school and how transsexuals' conditions affect careers. Childhood and the feelings transsexuals experience are explored in detail, as well as how the condition affects persons as they become adults. Many of the problems transsexuals have to cope with are examined, and the medical, surgical, and psychiatric care of transsexuals are all looked at in detail. What happens to transsexuals after they have surgery is probed. The subject of androgyny as it may relate to transsexualism is explored. The final chapter concerns the possible causes of transsexualism and how transsexuals and their loved ones can possibly find some common ground to understand each other. Throughout the book I discuss the attitudes and feelings transsexuals have, as well as how they are viewed by society and why.

All the names I use in the book are names I have chosen at random (unless I have quoted directly from another source) in order to protect the privacy of the men and women I talked to. Some of the persons I interviewed who may read this book will probably feel I am talking about them, in some cases. I must caution those readers, however, that I interviewed seventy-five persons, and many of the quotes I have included in this book were thoughts expressed to me by more than one person. I have used masculine names with masculine personal pronouns when talking about persons who identified themselves to me as female to male transsexuals. In the case of persons who identified themselves to me as male to female transsexuals, I have used feminine names and personal pronouns. I have made every effort to respect the privacy of individuals I interviewed, and any cross-reference to persons' real names has been destroyed. I have a list of those I interviewed, because I asked them all to sign releases before I interviewed them. I have no way of relating those names to individual interviews, however, or the fictitious names I have used.

This book is an attempt to better explain the condition of transsexualism on a realistic basis. The perspectives I gained from my research are reflected throughout the book. I have tried to be as objective as possible, and when I felt criticism was justified, I have leveled criticism. Readers should keep in mind that this is not a book of advocacy concerning transsexualism. Far from it. Throughout the book I have cautioned that the transsexual process is a treacherous path which can cause pain, suffering, and inflict deep emotional wounds. The book was written for the purpose of presenting the subject as it is experienced by transsexuals. There is a good deal of pain reflected in the book, because many transsexuals experience a lot of pain. The issues surrounding transsexualism are terribly complex, and I have tried to unravel those complexities and make them more understandable to all who are interested in this condition we call transsexualism.

**Kim Elizabeth Stuart**

# Chapter 1
# INTRODUCTION
# A COMMON VOCABULARY

### REBIRTH
Some years ago mother bore a boy
a child's mind as you may know
is always society's toy
I tried in vain to fit their mold
to my true self I was blind
A few of us can be so bold
to make gender self-define
A struggling woman's spirit
was desperate to be free
I tried so not to hear it
but I knew that she was me
I no longer lay my head sedated
on a pillow damp from crying
I have been reincarnated
without ever really trying.

This poem says in a very poignant way what this book is all about. It is about feelings: feelings people have who happen to be transsexuals.

The poem was read into my tape recorder at the end of an interview I had with a young woman while conducting research for this book. After the interviews were over, I usually asked the persons if they had any comments to add. This poem was her response.

When I started looking into the phenomenon of transsexualism, it seemed there was very little material available on the subject. There were several autobiographies by persons describing personal experiences. There also were some books written on the subject by physicians, psychiatrists, sociologists, and psychologists. While these personal accounts by former transsexuals and the books written by behavioral scientists who have dealt with transsexuals were useful, I could find almost nothing which looked at the subject from an overall perspective. Personal, anecdotal accounts and books written by professionals in specific fields can be very useful, but the persons writing them almost invariably narrow their focus. As we shall see, the condition of transsexualism is not just a medical problem, a psychological problem, a social phenomenon, or a singular experience. It is all of these and more.

As a writer, I felt there was a need to discuss the subject with the reading public and add another perspective to the body of literature concerning transsexualism. After reading as much as I could find on the subject and related matters, I devised a questionaire I felt would help me tell the story of transsexualism to the public. I wanted to broaden the focus and discuss it in a way that would demystify it, eliminate the sensationalism, and bring it into the mainstream of reality. It seemed to me, if those goals could be met, the public would come to understand transsexualism as an *uninvited dilemma*, and a *condition*, rather than a sensational sexual aberration only to be whispered or snickered about.

Through the help of several professionals who deal with transsexuals, I was able to contact a number of them. Overall, I conducted seventy five personal interviews. Each interview took from two to two and one half hours. All the interviews were tape recorded and I later transcribed them. Seventy of the interviews have been used in the statistical data which appears in a supplement to this book. Some of the interviews, which do not appear in the statistical data, were not used for one of several reasons. The interview is designed in such a way that conflicting answers quickly show up, and a few people were obviously not being truthful in their answers. One person, I later found out, completely fabricated the answers with no intention of telling the truth. A few others were very unresponsive to the questions. None of those interviews are included in the statistical data.

To balance the picture and be fair, it seemed to me, with the few exceptions I have mentioned, almost all the persons interviewed were very open and honest; they truly were interested in helping to educate the public concerning transsexualism.

I felt it would be helpful to make some comparisons, so I have divided the data into interviews between genetic male-to female transsexuals and genetic female-to-male transsexuals. There are fifty in the group of male-to-female, and twenty in the group of female-to-male. A more detailed explanation of the data appears at the beginning of the appendix.

Many of the books written by professionals who have dealt with transsexuals begin by tracing the history of the subject. Some books confine discussion to modern times, while others have made reference to figures throughout the history of mankind. Since the middle of this century when headlines carried the story of Christine Jorgensen, jokes about transsexuals have become a popular entree on the menu offered to the public by the comedians of our culture. Television talk shows have had a field day by dragging transsexuals across their stages.

Surrounding all this exposure, a body of myths has developed about transsexuals that has so distorted the picture, fiction has replaced fact in many persons' minds. My hope, in this book, is to explore the realities of transsexualism: Who are transsexuals? What do they think about themselves? Of others? Who deals with them and why? What do they have to go through, and what is that experience like? What sort of persons do they become? I am going to explore these issues, and some truths will probably be uncovered. In the process, the myths will take care of themselves. The scientific community is still uncertain as to what causes the condition of transsexualism. Though we must leave that explanation to them, I shall touch on various possibilities and theories. My purpose, however, is to deal with the realities as they exist for the persons involved.

I am not at all comfortable with labels, because they frequently promote unjust stereotypes. But many labels and terms are used by transsexuals and the persons who deal with them. Some readers may not be familiar with these terms, and I want to share with you the more frequently used terms; then we shall have a common vocabulary with which to discuss the subject.

In all cases, I shall try to define the terms in the manner I have come to understand them or how a dictionary would commonly define them. Some of the terms, I feel, after researching the subject for a year and one half, are not properly used or correctly defined. In these cases, I shall define them for you in the way they are commonly used, as well as how I feel they should be defined, or I shall give the reason why I feel they should not be used. In the body of the book I shall be consistent, and use those terms in the way I feel they should be applied; others I shall not use at all. There are two terms I shall be defining and using throughout the book which are not in common usage when transsexualism is discussed. I shall state the reasons I use them and why I feel they should be considered by others as I define them. All the terms I feel should be defined have been placed in alphabetical order so the reader can more easily refer to them while reading the book. They are also numbered to further facilitate reference.

1. *Being read.* This is a term which usually expresses fears transsexuals have when they try to present themselves to the public in roles opposite from their biological gender. It means transsexuals feel others are realizing they do not belong to the gender they are trying to present. I used the word fear, because in many cases persons who start to cross dress or cross-live are very self-conscious in the beginning. They fear anyone who happens to look at them knows the truth. In reality, most of us are somewhat preoccupied with our own lives, and not all that observant.

2. *Cross-dressing.* This means to wear clothing, privately or publicly, which is usually associated with persons of the opposite gender.

3. *Cross-living.* This means a person is living in a gender role opposite from his or her biological gender. I shall pick a name — any name — say, "Jane". When I say Jane is cross living, I mean Jane, who is a biological female, is living completely with a male identity. She takes on a male name, perhaps "Jack". If Jack works, he works with a male identity. All his identification is changed to indicate he is male. Jack presents publicly and socially as a male. All aspects of Jack's life are identified as male, with the exception of genitals.

4. *Former transsexual.* This is one of the terms I shall be using in the book which is not in common usage with reference to transsexualism. I would define a former transsexual as someone who has had surgery to alter his or her genitals to be more characteristic of persons of the opposite gender. Let me explain my thoughts about this phrase. The word trans is a Latin prefix which means across, beyond, through, so as to change. In modern English it means on, or to the other side of, across, beyond. Sexual is an adjective derived from the Latin sexualis, and it means of, relating to, or associated with sex or the sexes. When these two words are combined, the reason the term has been applied to some individuals becomes apparent.

Transsexuals must make many changes and overcome difficult obstacles. Somehow it seems unfair to burden people with labels which no longer seem appropriate when they have made changes, overcome obstacles, made adjustments, had surgery, and taken their places in society in roles in which they are comfortable. In their minds, it is no longer a question of being between or crossing between the sexes, as the term "transsexual" implies. And certainly, at that point, they have no desires to have surgical alteration of their genitals. If I need to refer to such individuals for the purpose of identification, I shall use the term "former transsexual."

5. *Gender*. This is a difficult term to clarify, because gender and sex are often synonymous in many persons' minds. Many books have been written on the subject of gender and sex. Historically, gender has been the means by which we classify biological sex (i.e., male or female). In language we have three genders, masculine, feminine, and neuter (i.e., it). In human beings and other animals, we assign only two genders, male and female. Sex relates to the reproductive organs, reproductive capabilities, or reproductive activities — in short the genitals, the function the genitals perform, and how the genitals are used for reproduction or pleasure.

Gender involves much more than the reproductive organs of males or females. It has social implications and involves many aspects of our lives which do not necessarily relate to genitals. Gender, it seems to me, is a more suitable term to use when discussing transsexualism, because sex is only one aspect of gender. Genetics reflect another feature of gender, as do the roles society assigns to males or females. By the time transsexuals are ready for genital surgery, many changes have already taken place. These persons are functioning hormonally, occupationally, emotionally, and socially in gender roles different from the roles they were assigned at birth. When surgery is completed, former transsexuals can function sexually in those congruent roles as well. If all this seems confusing, it really is not. Gender defines persons, and sex is a part of the definition. So, for the purpose of this book, I shall use the term gender, unless I am discussing specific sexual aspects of individuals.

6. *Gender community*. This term refers to the professionals who provide services for transsexuals, clinics which accept transsexuals, discussion groups, transsexuals themselves, and social groups formed where the basic common denominator is transsexualism. Frequently transvestites are included in these discussion and social groups. There is a good deal of confusion concerning the differences between transvestism and transsexualism amongst the general public, and within the gender community itself. Transvestism is dis-

cussed in some detail in Chapter 2, as are the differences between it and transsexualism.

7. *Gender congruity*. This is the other term I mentioned earlier which I prefer to use in place of more commonly used terms. Sex change, with the public, is a well-worn phrase describing gender congruity. Sex reassignment is the most common term which describes that congruity within the gender community. Many people believe what I term gender congruity is just a matter of surgical procedures being performed on transsexuals' genitals. This is not true; there are many steps involved. Transsexuals have to be evaluated and then treated medically with hormone therapy. Most male to female transsexuals have to undergo extensive electrolysis. All have to learn to adjust to roles opposite from those they were brought up in, learning to function in those roles occupationally, emotionally, and socially. Only then is surgery advised. Gential surgery is the last step following a long and arduous process. Gender reassignment might be a more appropriate term than sex reassignment, but I feel gender congruity best describes the entire process.

8. *Gender discomfort*. This phrase indicates a feeling of being ill at ease with one's gender of birth and all that implies.

9. *Gender dysphoria*. This term is frequently used to describe the condition transsexuals have by psychologists and psychiatrists. Dysphoria means hard to bear and hence, a state of feeling not well or happy. Persons who have gender dysphoria do not feel well or happy about their gender as assigned at birth. Gender dysphoria is the psychiatric term for gender discomfort.

10. *Gender identity*. Gender identity is twofold. It is the feeling all of us have of belonging to the male or female gender. In the case of transsexuals, the feeling of belonging is not compatible with the gender roles assigned to those persons at birth. The other side of gender identity is how other people identify us. The first thing we notice about persons is their gender. If their gender is not easy to determine, we look for whatever signs we can find to identify the gender of those persons. We find it difficult to concentrate on much of anything else about people until we are able to determine their gender, because we have a complicated and subtle set of determinants as to how we respond to persons, based not only on what their gender is, but what our own gender is as well. Gender is so basic to our identification of others that we almost never forget it, even if we remember little else about

them. Again, this is because we have very complex and varied ways of relating to others, depending on whether they are male or female, and whether we in turn are male or female.

11. *Gender roles.* Gender roles are what we might think of as societal expectations of how we are supposed to appear and behave in society, depending on whether we are male or female. Different cultures have different expectations for males and females, and role expectations change in some cultures over many generations.

12. *Post-operative transsexual.* This refers to a person who has had gential surgery to alter his or her sexual characteristics. I prefer and shall use the term former transsexual in this book.

13. *Pre-operative transsexual.* This is a person who has gender discomfort, but has not had surgery to alter his or her sexual characteristics.

14. *Sexual preference.* Sexual preference is who or what creates a sexual interest in persons. The "who" might be persons of the opposite gender, the same gender, or both. The "what", I suppose, could be animals, objects, or even circumstances. We certainly have examples of persons who enjoy having sex with non-human animals. We have heard of others who become fixated on certain objects such as women's underwear. Some pyromaniacs have masturbatory rituals with fire, and that constitutes a set of circumstances.

15. *Transsexual.* Definitions of this term are not at all uniform. Some define a transsexual as any person who has gender discomfort. Others only use the term in connection with a person who has had genital surgery (a former transsexual). Dictionaries vary widely when defining the term. It is little wonder that confusion is rampant concerning the subject of transsexualism. It would seem to me a simple, but appropriate definition is: A transsexual is a person who has a long-standing, internal image of possessing inappropriate sexual characteristics. Though it may not be definitive enough for some, or too inclusive for others, my research clearly indicates it is a valid definition.

We assign gender to persons at birth by viewing their genitals and labeling them male or female. Only if there are some biological anomalies would we consider investigating further and check the babies' chromosomes to verify genetic gender. Of course babies cannot speak for themselves at that time. In the pages ahead, the reader will discover, in most cases, transsexuals are not questioning their gender. What they question are the roles they have been placed in on the basis of their gentials. This is questioned because transsexuals do not feel comfortable in those roles.

# Chapter 2
# GENDER AND SEXUALITY

In the first chapter I pointed out that sex and sexuality are only components of gender. But there is no denying, in our everyday world, sexuality plays a very large role. Our sexual urges are perhaps most intense in early adulthood, but, excluding physical or emotional problems, we all have the potential to be sexually active from puberty to the end of our lives. The urges may not come as often, and the pleasures may not be as intense in our later years, but we can, as a rule, enjoy sexual activity in those later years. For many older persons, companionship and intimacy become a pleasant addition to sexual activity. Many have moved beyond the age of raising children or being as active in the work world as they once were.

We are all aware that reproduction is a key element of sexual activity. Some would argue on religious or moral grounds that reproduction is the only reason persons should engage in sexual activity. Their views, beliefs, and convictions should be respected. In contrast, others believe reproduction is only one of the functions of sexual activity. They feel the pleasure of sexual activity is just as important, if not more so, than reproduction. Their beliefs also deserve respect.

Modern science has given us a good deal of freedom with respect to reproduction. If religious or moral beliefs do not stand in our way, we have the ability, through contraception, to choose the number of children we want to raise and at what time of life we have those children. We also can elect not to have children at all. Science has carried us even further in reproductive freedom by the development of artificial insemination; sexual activity between men and women not even need occur in order to fertilize an egg. It seems astonishing that we now have the capability to fertilize an egg outside the body, implant the egg in a woman's uterus, and have it develop into a normal, healthy baby at birth. Fifty years ago such scientific developments were only the dreams of a few.

These scientific advancements have brought about a re-examination of sexual activity, and arguments rage in all di- 9 rections. Someone writes a book espousing open marriage; someone else advocates celibacy.

It seems to me, a certain amount of confusion concerning gender and sexuality results from not taking the time to make distinctions. In this chapter I want to separate and examine individually the differences between sexual preferences, sexual activities, sexual conditions, gender confusion, and gender discomfort. This book is about transsexualism, and I do not wish to dwell inordinately on sexual matters, but I feel that a key element to understanding what transsexualism really is rests with a clear awareness of, not only what these terms mean but what the differences between them are.

Everything I have been discussing so far with regard to sexual activity and sexuality concerns sexual relations between men and women. We must not overlook the fact that a significant portion of the population engages in sexual activities which are not heterosexual. I feel it is important to differentiate between sexual orientation and sexual activity. Sexual orientation falls into one of several catagories. The first is heterosexual. This refers to persons who are sexually aroused by persons of the opposite gender. Homosexual refers to persons who are sexually aroused by persons of the same gender. Bisexual describes those who are sexually aroused by persons of the male and the female gender. The term asexual describes persons who are not aroused sexually by either gender.

Sexual activities do not necessarily relate to sexual orientation. They describe the actions which take place when one or more persons become sexually aroused. Certainly sexual intercourse is the most common form of sexual activity between males and females, but it is by no means an exclusive activity. Non-coital copulation between the male sex organ and the female anal cavity is not at all unheard of, and oral-genital copulation between males and females is quite common. Non-coital anal copulation and oral-genital copulation are two forms of sexual activity commonly practiced by male homosexuals. Oral-genital copulation is a common sexual activity between female homosexuals. The list of possible sexual activites, however, whatever the orientation, is only limited by our imaginations and anatomies. Masturbation has to be considered a sexual activity and, as a rule, only one person is involved, but the slang expression "circle jerk" would indicate that it is not always an altogether singular activity.

Fantasies which may accompany masturbation might well involve others, objects, or circumstances.

Transvestism is a condition which is frequently misunderstood. It is commonly linked to transsexualism, because transvestites and transsexuals often cross-dress. Transsexualism may involve sexual orientation and sexual activity, but it revolves around gender discomfort. Transvestism also can relate to sexual orientation and to sexual activity. Gender confusion may be involved with either condition, but that is quite different from gender discomfort.

A transvestite is defined as a person who adopts the dress, and often the behavior of the opposite sex. I have serious reservations about this dictionary definition. Firstly, it uses the term opposite sex instead of opposite gender. Secondly, it only describes an activity and leaves to the imagination the motivation for the activity. In short, it describes a behavioral manifestation of a condition and fails to tell us the nature of the condition. It would be similar to describing apples as something people eat. That would not tell us anything about apples. Transsexuals frequently adopt the dress and often the behavior of the opposite gender. Many persons learn that transsexuals and transvestities cross–dress and incorrectly assume they are one and the same. This is what students of Aristotelian logic would term false logic. A syllogism is a form of reasoning which draws a deduction or conclusion by combining a major and a minor premise. I can best explain it by giving an example. If I state that grapefruit and oranges are citrus fruit, go on to say all citrus fruit grows on trees, I can come to a conclusion. If my premises are correct, I can logically deduce that grapefruit and oranges grow on trees, but — and I must emphasize this — I cannot re-arrange the formula to suit myself. For example, I cannot say that grapefruit grow on trees, go on to assert that oranges grow on trees, and then conclude grapefruit are oranges. In the same way, we cannot observe that transvestites cross dress, go on to note that transsexuals cross-dress, then conclude transvestites and transsexuals are one and the same. We would be coming to an incorrect conclusion based on a false syllogism. Correct logic can be reduced to numbers or symbols and proven mathematically; false logic cannot. It is not fair to transvestites or transsexuals to assume they are one and the same, or nearly the same, based on a particular activity they have in common. It also serves as a barrier to understanding either condition. When we make these kinds of assumptions, the

11

motivation for cross-dressing is overlooked, and that is the key to understanding both conditions.

I have described a transsexual as a person having a long-standing, internal image of possessing inappropriate sexual characteristics. Not so with a transvestite. Let a surgeon near a transvestite to alter his genitals, and he would probably set a world speed record going the other way.

A transvestite is a person who enjoys or becomes sexually aroused by wearing clothing of the opposite gender. Many transsexuals, at some point in their lives (usually just after puberty and beyond), become sexually aroused by wearing clothing of the opposite gender. This is by no means true, however, of all transsexuals. Again, let us beware of false logic.

Many people believe that transvestites are homosexual. The vast majority of them, however, are heterosexual. The homosexual transvestites are the ones the public most often see or hear about. These transvestites are sometimes exhibitionists and are homosexual males who dress in an effeminate manner. They usually cross-dress to attract other homosexual males who prefer effeminate males, and it is often their style of dress based on personal preferences. I use the word effeminate with deliberation, because most of these transvestites represent caricatures of women rather than trying to emulate women. They are frequently called drag queens, and some are professional female impersonaters.

The transvestites I have been describing are the type who usually draw public attention and, often, public disapproval. But make no mistake: these persons have no desires to alter their genitals, unless they have some gender confusion. Some will even go so far as to have breast implants but would never consider genital alteration.

Homosexual transvestites comprise only a small percentage of the transvestite population, but they are highly visible, and it is not uncommon for some to refer to themselves as transsexuals. If they are indeed transvestites, then of course they are not transsexuals. Many prefer the label because, in their eyes it seems to be a more legitimate condition, or they may feel it is more legitimate in the eyes of the public. Of course both conditions are legitimate, because they do exist. Whether or not the public approves of their conditions or the behavior they manifest, they have legitimate conditions. Some transvestites have gender confusion, and that subject is discussed in some detail in this and other chapters; gender confusion, however, is not to be understood to mean gender discomfort.

The transvestites who are least recognized and seldom understood are the ones who are heterosexual males. These transvestites make up most of the transvestite population. Transvestism does occur in genetic females, and I have talked to a few women who said they were transvestites, but it is rare. Most transvestites are men who become sexually aroused from wearing women's clothing, and some reach the point where they cannot be sexually aroused without cross dressing. Often, these transvestites say the clothing enhances their sexual experiences with their female partners. Unless you happen into an adult bookstore, or are a woman who discovers her mate likes to dress in female clothing at certain times, you do not hear much about by far the most common form of transvestism.

Most heterosexual male transvestites lead perfectly normal lives as males, to all intents and purposes. They are often very masculine in appearance and behavior. Only in the privacy of their homes or with groups which are formed to provide an opportunity to cross-dress does another side of their personalities emerge. Sometimes, women who are mates of transvestites will go along with cross-dressing habits, because they see it as harmless, or it sometimes enhances their sex lives. Other women feel threatened when their mates cross dress, and those transvestites have to seek pleasure cross dressing in secret at home or away from home.

Sometimes, heterosexual transvestism is linked to mild forms of sadomasochism. In pursuit of my research, I met a young woman by the name of Vickie who earns her living from transvestites. They come to her apartment, and Vickie dresses them in female clothing, sometimes ties them up or orders them about. Vickie told me a common fantasy of transvestites is to be dominated and/or humiliated by strong women. The humiliation, of course, is to be dressed in the clothing of what is considered the "weaker sex" and then ordered about. One Freudian explanation is that sexual arousal becomes a symbol to transvestites and, despite being dominated by females and, despite the humiliation of being dressed as women, they prove their superiority over women by being able to achieve erections. On the more practical side, Vickie told me this activity releases sexual energy, and the persons go on about their daily lives. Certainly not all transvestites carry their activities to this extreme, but it is not uncommon. Pictures and illustrations in magazines catering to transvestites often have sadomasochistic themes.

Many psychologists label transvestism as a sexual fetish. The dictionary defines a fetish in relation to sexuality as "an object or bodily part whose real or fantasied presence is psychologically necessary for sexual gratification and that is an object of fixation to the extent that it may interfere with complete sexual expression". We have all heard of what seem to be bizarre fetishes: men who become fixated on women's underwear or women's shoes. I have talked to a man who could only become sexually aroused and ejaculate in the proximity of fire. Although he is an arsonist, he is also one type of pyromaniac. He has an irrestible urge to set fires stemming from a deep-seated, sexual fixation.

Most arsonists are not pyromaniacs, of course, and most fetishes do not threaten others' lives. On the contrary, they are usually quite benign and provide sexual release for those involved. Whether there is a fixation on women's underwear, shoes, or wearing female clothing, those fetishes are sexual in nature and do not involve gender identity.

Some homosexual male transvestites do have gender confusion and occasionally may seek genital surgery in the belief they are transsexuals. Should they slip through a screening process, it is irreversible and tragic. Helen is a woman in her late thirties with whom I talked. She sought gender congruity surgery and received it. She felt that if her body and the role she played in society were changed, she could escape from emotional problems with which she had never learned to cope. "I used transsexualism to escape from the things that were happening in my life. I wanted to become a different person, and I found out afterwards that I wasn't a different person." Those are Helen's own words, not mine, and she said it better than I can describe it. She had not cross-lived prior to surgery and paid a dreadful price for not doing so. Only after the surgery had been performed did she realize she had been a very confused, homosexual male, and she still had all her original problems. Now she had a new and devastating one to add to the list. She was without the sexual characteristics which would allow her to participate in the gay world. Twice, after surgery, Helen attempted suicide. The second time she nearly bled to death after cutting her wrist. She was completely unconscious and without vital signs by the time she was taken to an emergency hospital. It has taken Helen years of psychotherapy to adjust to herself and her situation. Helen lives and, in the eyes of the world, copes in a female gender role. But, not unlike the man without a country, Helen wanders the world of sexuality — sentenced forever to sexual isolation — always searching, never belonging.

It is terribly important for physicians and therapists who may come into contact with transsexuals or persons who are convinced they are transsexuals, as Helen was, to understand the difference between gender confusion and gender discomfort. Some transvestites and homosexuals do have gender confusion. Judging by the persons I interviewed, most transsexuals at some point in their lives also have gender confusion. Usually by the time they acknowledge their situations and start making progress toward gender congruity, if that is their decision, the gender confusion passes, and only gender discomfort remains. Some transsexuals I interviewed never seemed to have much gender confusion and realized what they had to do at a very early age.

Gender confusion takes many forms, and my feeling is that if I confine it to a specific definition, some form of gender confusion might be overlooked. Confusion implies bewilderment, blurring, and the inability to make distinctions. Gender confusion, as I use the term in this book, refers to individuals who, for any number of reasons, simply have a difficult time establishing or maintaining a reasonably clear and comfortable identification with either the male or the female gender. Even that definition, however, does not entirely satisfy me. I do not want to establish perimeters with respect to this term, because inevitably someone would fall outside of those boundaries. I have just given a rather tragic illustration of gender confusion (Helen), and I write about others who have gender confusion in other chapters of this book. I feel the term, as I use it in the book, is best understood by means of illustration rather than definition.

Transvestites, in most cases, have sexual conditions, and some have gender confusion. In all cases, transsexuals have gender discomfort. They also may have gender confusion which may mask their gender discomfort. But gender confusion and gender discomfort must never be mistaken, for the sake of transvestites and the welfare of transsexuals. Sexual preference, on the other hand, is just that, and it exists in men and women whether they have gender conditions, sexual conditions, or neither.

Men and women who have gender conditions, sexual conditions, or sexual preferences different from most of the population are not necessarily emotionally ill. Family or societal pressures can and often do create emotional problems for these persons. We live in a complex society, and we are all vulnerable to emotional distress at various stages of our lives. If we cannot cope with that distress, we are certainly wise to seek help. Again, logic has to come into the picture, and it is important not to attribute cause and effect where it is not justified. Certainly those who have views, feelings which they act upon, or behavior patterns not considered normal by most of society are going to be vulnerable to emotional problems due to public and family disapprobation. But that is a far cry from labeling those views, feelings, or behavior sicknesses in and of themselves.

Transsexuals have gender conditions quite different from sexual conditions or sexual preferences. Transsexuals may, in addition to being transsexuals, have sexual conditions and sexual preferences considered abnormal by society as a whole. But that has nothing directly to do with their conditions of transsexualism. Unlike men and women who only have sexual conditions or sexual preferences, transsexuals usually need help, because they are very unhappy about the roles they have been forced to play in society due to their sexual characteristics. Most persons who have sexual conditions or sexual preferences do not want to make any changes in their lives, let alone their bodies, and they are perfectly content to be who they are. Transsexuals, on the other hand, usually want to make changes in their bodies and the gender roles they play in society. These changes require skilled, professional assistance. Transsexuals usually need help in determining how best to cope with their dilemmas, and should they decide to try the cross-living test, they often need support and guidance in learning to cope in roles they have not been raised in. It is one thing to feel that you will be comfortable in another role and quite another to adjust to that role. From the time we are born, we are treated quite differently, depending upon the gender role to which we are assigned. We are related to in very contrasting ways according to whether we are male or female, and we learn many subtle responses, attitudes, and behavior patterns in that socialization process. Most transsexuals have to make many adjustments to function successfully in other roles. Should transsexuals decide surgery is the best course of action to achieve gender congruity for them, they need highly skilled medical help for hormone therapy and, eventually, surgery.

In this chapter I have examined differences between gender discomfort, gender confusion, sexual conditions, sexual activities and sexual preferences. In summing this all up, it should be recognized that all transsexuals have sexual preferences, unless they happen to be asexual. Human beings are sexual creatures, so it would seem perfectly normal that different persons might have different sexual preferences and varying sexual conditions. Persons with gender conditions, sexual conditions, and sexual preferences also might have sexual problems that may or may not be related to their gender conditions, sexual conditions, or sexual preferences. What needs to be kept clearly in mind is that gender conditions, sexual conditions, sexual activities, and sexual preferences are all quite different subjects. We cannot just lump them all together and expect to have any real understanding of them.

# Chapter 3
# IN THE BEGINNING

When I designed the interview to provide research material, there were certain inherent problems I had to address. Firstly, I knew I would be interviewing a number of people who would be reluctant to share their personal experiences and feelings with a stranger. I knew I would have to earn their trust and felt the best way to do this would be to ask them questions about their families and other relationships. I hoped that if they had a chance to tell me about growing up with their families and the friends they had, they might become more comfortable. This seemed to be true. I gradually inserted questions about transsexualism as the interview progressed, and most persons responded positively to this approach.

The second major problem I faced was to determine how I wanted to use the material I would be gathering. One choice would have been to conduct a major statistical study of transsexuals and their lives. Certainly that would have been a very useful and valid study. In order to do that, however, I would have had to use a control group of men and women who were not transsexuals. The alternative, as I saw it, was to find out as much as I could about transsexuals, their feelings and experiences, and write the book based on what I learned. The first choice intrigued me, as I always have had an interest in sociology, but the second alternative appealed to me more as a writer.

The more I wrestled with this problem, the more I came to realize some sort of compromise would have to be reached. It became obvious that for many of the questions a control group would not be possible. One cannot compare an experience to a non-experience. How does one compare a feeling to a non-feeling? Many of the experiences transsexuals encounter and the feelings they have are unique to transsexuals; it would seem futile to contrast them to persons who have not had comparable experiences and feelings. On the other hand, valid comparisons can be made in some areas. As an example, eighty-five percent of the persons I interviewed told me their parents did not communicate well with them, if at all, about personal matters such as feelings, sex, and relationships. This figure seems very high to me, and I wonder how it compares to the general population. Does only one in seven persons receive any real sexual and social education in the home? Just over seventy-five percent of all the persons I interviewed had one or more years of college, yet almost forty-three percent of those persons interviewed indicated they were not happy in their present careers. Twenty-eight percent had performed mostly unskilled labor in their adult lives, and thirty-five percent were unemployed at the time of the interview. Again, these percentages seem high to me. Many questions, such as these, come to mind when reading the questions and answers. Some can be answered in this book, but many cannot; they deserve investigation by social scientists.

In the end, I decided I did not want to conduct a statistical study of transsexuals' lives. I placed the statistical data in a supplement to this book and only will refer to it as a backdrop in discussing transsexualism. I am much more interested in telling the story from the point of view of experiences and feelings. I intend to use the research data primarily as an aid to illustrate points and emphasize feelings expressed to me by those men and women I interviewed. Some of the data is unique in that it cannot be compared to figures from the general population, and I will certainly be commenting on that information. I have, in effect, married the information I have compiled statistically to the experiences, feelings, and stories people have told me. This is why with few exceptions I have not referred to books on the subject of transsexualism by other authors. Those books present the authors' perspectives, but my purpose in writing this book is to present the perspectives I gained from talking to transsexuals.

No attempt was made by me to record racial, ethnic, or religious backgrounds. Since I was not setting out to uncover possible environmental causes of transsexualism, I felt such material would be of little use to me. It is of interest, however, that I interviewed transsexuals who were of white, American Indian, black, and Oriental descent. Ethnically, there was tremendous diversification. I talked to people who had been raised in Western Europe, Australia, the South Pacific and a wide variety of ethnic backgrounds throughout the United States. I interviewed Jews, Catholics, Mormons, born-again Christians, Protestants, Buddhists, cultists, agnostics, and atheists. In short, the men and women I talked to were a microcosm of our society racially, ethnically, and religiously.

The persons I interviewed came from a wide variety of economic backgrounds. Overall, about forty—one percent came from middle income families. There is one interesting disparity between the two groups with respect to economic backgrounds. Almost twice as many male to female transsexuals came from upper-middle income to wealthy families as did female to male transsexuals. This may or may not be significant, but the answers to the questions raised by these figures lie in research, not speculation.

The oldest transsexual I interviewed was sixty-nine, and the youngest was twenty-two. Wilma, the sixty-nine year old transsexual, had been married until her former wife was unexpectedly killed in an automobile crash. Wilma told me she had feelings she should have been a woman all her life, but she never did anything about them because she had a family, and a reasonably compatible marriage. Of course when Wilma grew up and became a young adult, there was not even a word for transsexualism; even if she had wanted to do something about her situation, there was no help available. Wilma now feels that since she no longer has family responsibilities, she is free to pursue a path she might have followed had it been open to her at an earlier age.

The average age was about thirty-four, but it is interesting to note that female-to-male transsexuals seem to start acknowledging their situations and start trying to deal with them a little earlier in life than do the male-to-female transsexuals. Most female-to-male transsexuals seem to take positive steps to cope with their dilemmas from their mid-twenties to mid-thirties, while most of the male-to-female transsexuals seem to start dealing with their dilemmas in their late twenties and beyond.

The number of female-to-male transsexuals I was able to contact for interviews was a little more than one out of three in ratio to the male to female group. In past years, it was speculated that the national average was about one female to male transsexual to every four male-to-female transsexuals. Paul Walker, Ph.D, a noted psychologist who specializes in gender and sexual problems, has indicated that presently the number of female-to-male transsexuals coming forward is very nearly equal to the number of male-to-female transsexuals. Dr. Walker is certainly in a position to make such a judgment. He worked actively in San Francisco, California with transsexuals and was on the staff of Johns Hopkins University from 1969 to 1976. It was there the first male-to-female gender reassignment surgery was performed in the United States in 1965. He was the Director of the Gender Clinic at the University of Texas Medical Branch at Galveston, Texas, from 1976 to 1980. Dr. Walker was instrumental in helping to found the Harry Benjamin International Gender Dysphoria Association, as well as the standards of care that organization developed. He enjoys a worldwide reputation for his research as well as his clinical experience.

So much publicity surrounded persons such as Christine Jorgensen and others that little publicity was given to the condition of female-to-male transsexualism in years past. Recently, however, the media has spotlighted female-to-male transsexuals, and that is perhaps why more of them are coming forward. Many of the female-to-male transsexuals I interviewed told me that even though they compared their dilemmas to someone such as Christine Jorgensen, they just had no idea anything could be done to help them.

"I was pretty much of a loner" is a phrase which was repeated to me over and over when I asked persons whether they enjoyed relationships with other kids as they were growing up. Valerie, a former male-to-female transsexual, expressed her feeling in this way: "I wanted relationships desperately, but I felt like an outsider looking in. I knew, at a very early age, I was different from the other boys." Ike, a female-to-male transsexual, experienced relationships somewhat differently. "I felt I threatened the boys, because I was as aggressive as they were. I attracted girls, almost as in boy-girl relationships, and then they would hate me for drawing them into those types of relationships. I just didn't have any close friends, and I wasn't at all popular."

These two experiences seem to be fairly typical of the feelings many transsexuals had in childhood. Most of the persons I interviewed did not feel they were popular in primary and secondary schools. Most did not have very many friends, because they felt alienated, or did not want to get too close to contemporaries for fear their secrets would be discovered. Ida, a male-to-female transsexual, put the former feeling this way: "I tried to be like the other kids, but there was just always something about me the other kids picked up on right away." Ken, a female-to-male transsexual, expressed the latter feeling when he said, "I was always afraid that if I got too close to any of the other kids, they might discover my secret. Adults didn't talk all that much about things like sex the way kids did, so I always felt safe around adults." Fifty eight and one-half percent of the men and women I interviewed said they got along better with adults and felt more comfortable with them than with their peers. That certainly seems to validate the feelings Ken expressed to me.

It is not surprising that many transsexuals grow up feeling alienated from their peers. Almost always, transsexuals believe they are the only persons in the world who have the feelings they have. Many of them are just not able to conform to their gender roles effectively, so it is not uncommon for them to be teased and bullied by schoolmates and other kids in their neighborhoods. An extremely high percentage of transsexuals I interviewed experienced periods of abnormal introversion and withdrawal. They would come straight home from school, stay in their rooms, and virtually eliminate social intercourse from their lives. This period of withdrawal frequently came about between the sixth and ninth grades. It is certainly not difficult to understand why this might happen at that stage of life. This is the period when boys and girls start to become very socialized in gender roles and aware of their bodies as well. Boys and girls start engaging in activities which are more common to their gender roles at that point and become more we-they oriented. Boys and girls become pubescent in this age span usually, and sexuality spawns from mild curiosity into urgent intensity. Certainly if boys or girls have gender discomfort at this point, they are quite likely to feel totally alienated from the process and choose to drop out.

Most of the persons I interviewed seemed to come out of their withdrawal after they had been in high school for a while or, if they went to college, not long after they entered college. This would seem plausible, because as we approach adulthood, more emphasis is placed on judging persons by their abilities and personalities, rather than on their appearances or eccentricities. Many persons told me that once they enrolled in college, the atmosphere was much more open, and less judgmental. Their spectrum of friends also widened, so they were able to meet more people who had similar interests and tastes.

Nick, a female-to-male transsexual, was literally forced into withdrawal. His father took him to school in the mornings and picked him up after school, so Nick was never allowed to mingle with schoolmates in leisure time. He was not allowed out of the house in the afternoon until he had finished his homework. Nick was an honor student, and he seldom finished his homework before supper. He was forbidden to leave the house and play with neighborhood children after supper, so Nick was brought up in virtual social isolation from his contemporaries. It is, of course, not surprising that Nick grew up with tremendous emotional problems quite aside from his condition of transsexualism. Nick, who is in his forties, is just beginning to learn to cope with his problems and find some meaning to his life. Until now, Nick has never had a fulltime job in his life, yet he has a bachelor's degree in Biology and studies such things as calculus to amuse himself. At the time I interviewed Nick he was taking a course in computer programming. Several months after the interview, he called to tell me he had found a job with a large electronics firm. The feeling of pride and self-worth I could hear in his voice was heartwarming. Nick has put his life together socially and economically, and he is now dealing with his condition of transsexualism. For the first time in over forty years, Nick is enjoying the sweet taste of life.

The reader may be wondering what Nick's story has to do with the subject of transsexualism. His story is bizarre and relatively rare, but it does dramatically emphasize the fact that persons can grow up being transsexuals and have emotional problems which have little relationship to those persons' transsexualism. Most transsexuals, and most persons in society, do not grow up under the circumstances Nick faced. But many persons who happen to be transsexuals do grow up and develop emotional problems which may not be related directly to their transsexual conditions. Of course problems frequently overlap, and it is often difficult to sort them out without some professional help. Helen, the woman I talked about in Chapter 2, learned the hard way that she could not run away from herself in order to escape her problems. It is very important for transsexuals and the physicians and therapists who may deal with them to realize that emotional problems not necessarily related to gender discomfort should have a high priority. If these problems are not resolved, gender confusion is often difficult to separate from gender discomfort.

The condition of transsexualism has tremendous impact on the persons involved, but the way it affects their loved ones is seldom talked about. I was a little surprised when I compiled the statistics to find that about forty percent of the mothers of male-to-female transsexuals supported the decision to seek gender congruity. Even more surprising was the 23 fact that almost sixty percent of the fathers were supportive. The figures were a little lower for the female-to-male transsexuals, although, as with male-to-female transsexuals, fathers were more supportive than mothers. Thirty-seven percent of the mothers were supportive, while about forty-three percent of the fathers were supportive. Unlike many parents, brothers and sisters had a very low ratio of support. Twenty-six percent of the brothers and sisters of male-to-female transsexuals were supportive, while only eighteen percent of the brothers and sisters of the female-to-male group were supportive. These figures seem understandable in that parents would be more likely to accept their children, "no matter what", than would their brothers and sisters.

Many transsexuals enter the adult world, get married, and have children. Some transsexuals do this in the belief that marriage and a family will resolve their gender discomfort, and some do it because of family and societal pressures. Older transsexuals who grew up prior to the nineteen fifties and sixties did not have psychological services and surgical techniques available to help them with their dilemmas. They, as most persons in society, wanted relationships and families. Since they could not get married and have families in any but the gender roles which they were assigned at birth, they did so in those gender roles. That is perhaps why we see older transsexuals coming forth rather late in life now that help is available to them.

Whatever the reasons, many transsexuals do get married and have families prior to pursuing gender congruity. It was a surprise to learn that just over fifty percent of the spouses, or former spouses, of the transsexuals in my study were supportive of those persons seeking gender congruity. When it comes to children, my study showed a marked contrast between spousal support of the male-to-female transsexuals, and the female-to-male transsexuals. Sixty-three percent of the former spouses of male-to-female transsexuals provided such encouragement. Hal (Barbara is her given name) told his spouse he wanted to seek gender congruity. The husband flew into a rage and told Hal that if he ever did such a thing he would take Hal's children away from him, and he would never see them again. Hal (Barbara) is the natural mother of those children (again, throughout this book I always refer to persons in the masculine gender with a masculine name, if they identify themselves to me that way, and I always refer to persons in the feminine gender with a feminine name, if they identify themselves to me as male-to female transsexuals). Rather than take a chance on losing his children, Hal has decided not to do anything about his gender discomfort. Hal loves his children very deeply, and his decision is certainly understandable. It does seem a shame, however, that he has to go through life knowing his gender discomfort could be alleviated but afraid to take those steps for fear of losing the ones he cares most about.

Almost ninety percent of the male to female group had support from some of their children, while about sixty-six percent of the female to male group had the support of some of their children. In general, it would seem children of transsexuals are by far more supportive of those persons seeking gender congruity than are their parents, their brothers and sisters, or their former spouses. We must remember, however, that gender identity is deeply rooted in our culture; it is not easy for parents, children, brothers, sisters, spouses, and friends who always have known someone in one gender role to accept a shift in gender identity. We have to sympathize with their dilemmas as well as with those transsexuals encounter. Many transsexuals told me their loved ones just could not or would not try to cope with the situation. There is also a deeply ingrained homophobia in our culture and, unfortunately, many people equate transsexualism with homosexuality. They do not distinguish between gender roles, gender identity, and sexual preference. This is due of course to a lack of information and a totally inadequate job of public education about transsexualism.

In Chapter 2, I pointed out that gender conditions are quite different from sexual conditions or sexual preferences. The word *transsexual* is somewhat misleading, because the word *sexual* is incorporated into the term. Perhaps the word "transgender" would have been a more suitable term, but I say that in hindsight. It seems clear to me from reading the early literature that the full scope of transsexualism was not understood, and it was considered more of a sexual condition than a gender condition. The average person has only been exposed to the sensationalism surrounding transsexualism. It is not surprising, therefore, that when someone finds out a person he or she has known for many years is a transsexual, and wants gender congruity surgery (sex change surgery as it is almost always referred to by the media), to assume that the person must be a homosexual. I will be discussing the subject of sexual preference as it relates to transsexuals in Chapter 6, but anyone who reads the supplement which is available to this book will discover that transsexuals have diverse sexual preferences in the gender roles they wish to adopt. Since human beings are sexual by nature, we all have sexual preferences, regardless of our gender roles. Most psychiatrists and psychologists now recognize that sexual preferences different from the norm are not sicknesses, and they are not something which can be changed by therapy.

Gender identity is a completely separate issue from sexual preference. The majority of persons in our society, of course, are heterosexual. If that were not the case, the human race would soon disappear. The majority of transsexuals are also heterosexual. As in the general population, however, some are homosexual, some are bisexual, and I interviewed a few transsexuals who were totally asexual. Again, the misunderstanding probably stems from confusing gender conditions and sexual preferences. As I have pointed out, persons may have the sexual characteristics of the male gender and yet those persons may have personal gender identities as females. If those persons have always felt they had inappropriate sexual characteristics, had internal identification as females all their lives, and proceed with genital surgery to obtain sexual characteristics appropriate to females, it makes absolutely no sense to classify those persons as homosexuals if they prefer male sexual partners. Some former male to female transsexuals do prefer female sexual partners, and these women are indeed homosexuals. But if persons have played unwanted male gender roles and shift their gender identities to female, they will prefer male sexual partners if they are heterosexual. The reverse is true in the case of female-to-male transsexuals.

A by-product of the research I did for this book was the perspective I gained from getting to know some of the families and friends of those I interviewed. Time and again, transsexuals I interviewed expressed concern and a certain amount of anger which was directed toward loved ones who could not understand their plights. Some parents and loved ones, I discovered, were actually unequivocal in their support and understanding. The mother of one male-to-female transsexual I interviewed told me that it did not make any difference to her whether Adelle was male or female. She said she just loved Adelle and wanted her to be comfortable and happy. A number of parents even go to the hospital with their children at the time of their surgeries, as did Adelle's mother. All these parents are supportive, even if they do not fully understand why their children need to do such things. They love their children too much to let shifts in gender roles interfere with their love. A number of former spouses are also quite supportive of transsexuals. In some cases, the couples are so devoted that even though they may obtain divorces, they plan on living together after the transsexuals have surgery.

Now all this support sounds ideal, and it is when it happens. But for many others, the decision to seek gender congruity leaves a trail of broken hearts, shame and, frequently, hate in its path. Though many transsexuals do not understand why loved ones cannot sympathize with their dilemmas, it is, at best, a very bitter pill for many to swallow. Some parents blame themselves for something they feel they must have done when raising their children to have those persons become transsexuals. Instead of trying to cope with the situation and salvage their love of those persons, they find it easier to anguish in their own guilt. That guilt, not infrequently, turns to shame, and often they cannot discuss the subject between themselves, let alone with others. Many former spouses also experience various forms of guilt. Some question their own masculinity or feminity and blame themselves for not being able to continue to attract their mates. Others experience a deep sense of shame and diminishment of self-worth, because they feel they must have used very poor judgment in their choices of marriage partners. On the other hand, some loved ones, rather than feeling guilt, blame the transsexuals, and this all too often turns to contempt and hatred. Those loved ones feel transsexuals have betrayed them, rather than having done something to relieve their discomfort. They usually do not understand what transsexualism is and frequently they are unwilling to even learn. They feel the transsexuals have cavalierly betrayed them, and they have no right to pursue gender congruity because it hurts others. I cannot respond to those feelings from the point of view of transsexuals or loved ones who feel betrayed. Both have legitimate feelings, and I am not sure any of us have a right to sit in judgment. Transsexuals and the loved ones who feel betrayed have very real feelings, and valid reasons for those feelings, in their eyes. One can only wish for common sense to prevail in such situations. Minds can guide hearts, and hearts can guide minds, but love is finite since human beings in the world are finite, and I wonder if any of us have the right to question, let alone pass judgment, on others' love or lack of it. I think maybe we have to be satisfied with the love we do find and are capable of giving without finding fault with others because their capacity to love and be loved does not meet our standards.

Although many former spouses of transsexuals are supportive, many others are not. It is not uncommon for some former spouses to react in hysterical ways, and if children are involved, they may go so far as to take the children away from transsexuals and deny them any possibility of relationships with the children.

Even if a former spouse is quite supportive and there is a small child involved, some confusion is bound to result in that child's mind. When a young child starts to learn about life, and the differences between boys and girls, this is a very vulnerable stage in the child's life. A young boy or girl does not conceptualize in the same way adults are capable of doing about such things as gender roles. Children think more directly, and they learn that there are mommies and daddies; that mommies and daddies often perform different tasks (depending on their particular family environment); mommies and daddies dress differently; mommies have breasts, daddies do not; daddies have penises, mommies do not. This is the way small children first learn about family relationships. If a mommy or daddy should make a decision to shift gender roles, there has to be a certain amount of confusion in a youngster's perceptions. Even if both parents are supportive and explain as best they can what is happening, some bewilderment is inevitable. No matter if the child becomes totally supportive of the transsexual parent, that child has to deal internally as well as externally with what happened to mommy or daddy. I think any psychologist who deals with children would agree that such a child is more at risk of developing future psychological problems than most children. The key, I should think, would be how the child is able to cope internally, and eventually outwardly, with the loss of mommy or daddy, even if he or she maintains a loving relationship with the transsexual parent in another gender role. Friends of the child will have parents with male and female identities, even if the parents are divorced or one of them is no longer living, and a common way for a child to cope with the loss of a transsexual parent in his or her original gender role is to think of that parent as having died, in terms of the gender role. That is not to say children cannot continue to have loving relationships with transsexual parents; they can and often do. How children cope with the loss of the parents in their original gender roles is what children are dealing with, not the transsexual parents as persons. Early on, a child learns that there are two gender roles, male and female. The concept of transsexualism, at best, is difficult for most adults to comprehend, let alone a child. When a youngster is just starting to understand what life is all about, in terms of gender roles and identifying himself or herself as male or female, it has to be very bewildering if he or she is confronted with a transsexual parent who elects to seek gender congruity. On the other hand, children are marvelously adaptable; and if the situation is handled with gentleness and care by both parents, the young child may well survive without any psychological damage. It certainly should be incumbent on both parents, however, to be on the lookout for any danger signals; and if they should flash, see that the child is provided with professional help.

At best, relationships with loved ones and transsexuals is a very mixed bag. I cannot think of any one, dramatic revelation which would help to improve relationships. It certainly seems a shame so many opportunities for love are lost because of the dilemmas transsexuals find themselves in. A great number of the persons I interviewed have had surgery since I interviewed them, and many have kept in contact with me. Although some of them perhaps were not adequately prepared psychologically, most certainly seem to be far more comfortable with themselves, and they are probably more interesting persons to know than before they had gender congruity surgery. Many loved ones miss out on the richest time of former transsexuals' lives, and that seems a terrible waste. The only solution which I feel will help to alleviate the problem is for our society to learn more about the condition of transsexualism. In the process, persons will probably become less judgmental and capable of continuing their love of persons in other gender roles. Many of the problems transsexuals have result from a lack of acceptance, but that is a two-way street. Transsexuals have no more right to demand acceptance than loved ones have to demand transsexuals not be allowed to deal with their dilemmas. Love and acceptance are not commodities, and they cannot be bought and sold. Certainly no one has the right to demand them, because they are gifts which only can be given by human beings freely. Patience, understanding, truth, and knowledge will do more to help everyone cope with transsexualism than fear, shame, and ignorance. The former lead to a path of love, while the latter lead us down a twisted, cluttered trail of bitterness and hate. The brambles of hate scratch and tear at the mind, and fear of the unknown lies around each turn.

# Chapter 4
# GOING TO SCHOOL AND WORKING

At the time I was conducting interviews, I recall telling personal friends that the persons I was interviewing, by and large, seemed to be quite intelligent. The statistics certainly would seem to verify that impression. Seventy percent of the female-to-male transsexuals I interviewed had at least one year of college. Thirty-five percent of that group had at least a bachelor's degree, and fifteen percent of the entire group had advanced degrees. The figures were even higher in the male-to-female group. Seventy-eight percent of them had at least one year of college; forty-two percent had at least a bachelor's degree, and sixteen percent had advanced degrees.

These figures, I am sure, are much higher than the educational level of the general population in this country. I know of no statistics concerning the educational levels of transsexuals, although there may be a study I have not come across. Racially, ethnically, religiously, and economically the persons I interviewed came from all walks of life. The only explanation I can think of for this educational variance is that more persons volunteered for interviews who had higher educational levels simply because they were interested in helping to inform the public about the subject. This would seem perfectly logical in that the more education persons have, the more likely they would be to realize the impact public education would have for themselves and other transsexuals. I solicited interviews through therapists and physicians who deal with transsexuals individually and in groups. The fact that these persons were looking for help in such a manner would indicate to me they were searching for intelligent ways of coping with their dilemmas. Although I did interview some persons who might be classified as street people, there are countless transsexuals who are just living their lives and do not look for help through individual therapy, group therapy, or rap groups. Many are extremely poor; some turn to prostitution, crime, and drugs. The cross living experience, at best, is often a very difficult period for transsexuals, because their appearances and behavior are somewhat androgynous in the beginning; therefore, it is very difficult for these persons to earn their livings in socially acceptable ways. The less education they have, the more difficult their positions become. They, as do other minorities, often become alienated from the mainstream of society when poverty, poor education, and inequality whirls them around in vicious circles. These persons become bitter and hostile, and often exhibit socially unacceptable behavior, which in turn brings down the wrath of society on them even harder, and around and around they go.

There is a very interesting anomaly which appeared in the statistics regarding education. One of the questions I asked was as follows: "Did gender discomfort ever cause you any academic problems at school (i.e., difficulty in concentrating)?" Thirty percent of the female to male group responded "yes" to this question while twice that many in the male to female group answered "yes". Although gender discomfort interfered with academic performance in a significant number of female-to-male transsexuals, it seems to have affected the grades of almost two-thirds of the male-to-female group. I can think of only one plausible explanation for such a large differential. Our society, in general, seems to be more tolerant of young girls dressing and behaving in ways usually associated with boys than of boys dressing or behaving in ways usually associated with girls. We have no equivalent word for tomboy in reference to boys. The closest thing to it would be sissy, and that, of course, carries a very negative connotation. Most parents are just slightly amused at young, tomboy daughters and assume they will outgrow the stage. If a young boy, however, exhibits comparable behavior, all sorts of red flags go up, and nobody is in the least amused. It well may be that young girls are allowed enough latitude with respect to dress and behavior that gender discomfort is not such an important factor in their lives as it is for boys during the school years (at least in terms of being able to concentrate on schoolwork). This however, was not true for Ike, a female-to male transsexual. Ike told me: "I burned up a tremendous amount of time and energy thinking about my transsexualism, and I found it difficult to concentrate on other things".

Ike's comments, in general, were actually very typical of many of the male-to-female experiences. Evelyn: "It affected my grades in terms of my being able to concentrate." Gail: "I mostly wanted to stay home and cross-dress, and this affected my grades." Margaret: "I was standoffish with other students, preoccupied looking at girls, and envying them, and it took much time away from my studies." Pam: "The knowledge that my transsexualism was going to surface sooner or later was always on my mind, and I used up a lot of energy thinking about that." Susan: "Most of my energy in school was devoted to envying girls and wanting to be part of their world. I found it very difficult to concentrate on schoolwork. My mind was constantly preoccupied with my secret desire in school and at home. Of course I couldn't tell any of my friends how I felt. I tried to be somewhat macho to make up for my feelings, and so no one would find out my real secret. I guess people mostly thought I wasn't very smart, because I seemed to be one of the boys but got very poor grades. The whole thing was a terrible waste and just a part I played to guard my secret."

The ways Ike, Evelyn, Pam, and Susan experienced gender discomfort in relation to their schoolwork was very typical of many transsexuals, but the diversification of the human mind is a wonderful thing, and others dealt with gender discomfort in quite another way. Art: "It turned me into an over-achiever. Since I couldn't excel at sports like the boys, at least I could be somebody academically." Carol: "Transsexualism probably helped my grades, because I found an outlet to avoid dealing with it through achieving." So, while gender discomfort greatly interfered with most transsexuals' schoolwork, it provided some with an arena to be stars, or a means of not having to think about their discomfort by concentrating on studying.

Gender discomfort seems to have caused a lot of mischief in the academic lives of transsexuals, but, in terms of their social lives and social development as boys and girls, it had a devastating effect. Almost eighty percent of those I interviewed told me they had tremendous difficulties relating to other kids when they were in school. Most felt very alienated and, as I observed in Chapter 3, many became very introverted and withdrawn during their growing years. Gail put it this way: "I played the game of being normal and functioned, but it was difficult for me to be close to anyone." Pam: "It caused me to consider all the activities I was supposed to participate in and view them as sort of a spy who really shouldn't be there." George: "In school, everything was backwards for me socially from the time I was in about the second grade." Susan expressed her feelings this way: "I tried to be one of the guys. I played a lot of sports, and was pretty good at them. I found physical activity released a lot of 33 energy for me I wasn't able to use studying, but my mind wandered right back to my dilemma when I wasn't active physically. I played the part, had crushes on girls, bragged to the other guys about making out and, outwardly, was interested in most of the things guys are supposed to be interested in. My voice became very deep, and that helped to put over the masculine image. I just didn't know of any other way to cope with my feelings, because I felt very guilty for feeling the way I did."

Again, transsexuals seemed to have responded to social situations as boys and girls in many diverse ways. Some withdrew, some acted the part out, and others, who tried to participate, were not very convincing in their assigned gender roles. The latter took terrible beatings emotionally and, not infrequently, physically. Art became the class clown. "They couldn't take me too seriously about anything, so I was able to stay at a distance from the other kids." Carol became the class sissy and was continually teased and beaten up by the other boys in school. Dorothy, on the other hand, became a rebel and continued to flaunt cross-dressing in front of her parents. "I became difficult to handle, and my parents sent me to a school which specialized in emotionally disturbed children to cure me of my cross-dressing. They put me in macho situations (such as the boys' dormitory with the reputation for having the toughest boys in it) to masculinize me, and I was heavily tranquilized. After two years, the school gave up on me and told my parents there was nothing they could do."

Most transsexuals survive childhood, as do other boys and girls. Eventually they come into adulthood, face career choices, and confront economic pressures. Just about seventy five percent of the persons interviewed had at least one or more years of college. Out of that seventy-five percent, over fifty-two percent had bachelor's degrees, and almost forty percent of those who had bachelor's degrees had advanced degrees. Despite this very high level of education, almost thirty-five percent of the persons I interviewed were unemployed at the time of the interviews. Of those who were employed, about fifty-five percent of them indicated they were not particularly happy about the work they were doing and wanted to enter another career. Forty-two percent also indicated they would like to have a career which did not seem realistic in terms of their education or work experience. These are sobering and frightening statistics. A thirty-five per-

cent unemployment ratio amongst any group of people is

staggering, and indicative of a serious social situation. While it is true transsxuals comprise only a tiny fraction of less than one percent of the total population, they are, nevertheless, human beings with abilites, needs and, in many cases, families to support.

Carl is a good example of what happens to many transsexuals. He moved to California from the south, because he had heard there was more professional help and support services available for transsexuals in California than in other areas of the United States. He gave up an interesting, good paying, white-collar job in a large southeastern city to move to California in order to find help with his transsexual dilemma. Carl has a master's degree in his field, but he has had to work at jobs outside of his field paying not much more than minimum wage since he has lived in California. He started cross-living as a man when he moved to California. He also started on hormone therapy at that time. As a consequence, and for a number of months, Carl presented a very androgynous appearance, and potential employers simply did not want to give him a chance. Carl has had a difficult time getting some of his records changed to present his new gender role, and his former employer would not give him references reflecting his new identity. Carl is slowly getting on his feet, but he has had to make terrific financial and career sacrifices in order to resolve his gender discomfort.

Valarie, a former male-to-female transsexual, has had an equally difficult time. "I was very successful in a very specialized selling field, and my future seemed unlimited. I had a smart, beautiful wife and two lovely children, but when I was about twenty-eight my transsexualism caught up with me, and I became consumed by it. My sales production fell off, but my firm was very patient with me. They tried to help me and find out what was interfering with my work, because I had such an outstanding record with them. Of course I was ashamed to tell them what my problem was, and they eventually had to let me go. Now that I have dealt with the problem of transsexualism and had surgery, I am trying to rebuild my life. I'm glad I did what I did, because I feel comfortable with myself for the first time that I can remember, but it's been tough. I have no references in the female role and don't have the love of my family to keep me going. I think I'm going to make it, but it won't be easy."

The experiences of Carl and Valarie are very typical of what many transsexuals go through. I pointed out earlier that many transsexuals develop a great deal of social dysfunction in childhood. Certainly these problems often carry over into adulthood, and it is not uncommon for these disturbances to compound career problems. Many transsexuals, unless they are very good at acting, tend to live in shells. They protect their secrets from the world by shutting it out, except for minimal needs, and, because they are often intent on protecting their feelings, it is not uncommon for some to develop symptoms of paranoia. When all these social and emotional problems are accentuated by a period of androgyny and difficulty in obtaining valid legal identity, transcripts, records, references, and employment, it becomes quite difficult for many transsexuals to function in any capacity. Many who do not have the financial and emotional resources to cope with such a myriad of problems turn to drugs, and wind up on the fringes of society.

Many transsexuals do find their way through the maze I have been describing, and then they must deal with life as men and women. Many former female-to-male transsexuals find, to their surprise in some cases, that life is no easier for men than it is for women, and some male-to-female transsexuals begin to understand a little more fully what equal rights is really all about. It is one thing to observe the opposite gender from the sanctity of one's personal gender identity, but is quite another to experience it. When, for example, I interviewed Adam, he was beginning to understand a little better what being a male in our society is really like. "Lately, I have been feeling some of the pressures of male expectation to have a hotshot job and be successful. I realize it's a trap, but I feel the pressures. I have a problem with whether I want to climb the corporate ladder and conform." Adam, in a real sense, was experiencing one of the realities of being male in our corporate society; something, incidently, far removed from his sexuality. This again emphasizes the thrust of my earlier discussion concerning sexuality and gender and is exactly why I find a sexual definition of men and women to be one-dimensional. It only describes one aspect — admittedly an important one — of what a male or a female is. Gender is multi-dimensional, and describes the whole person, not just his or her sexual nature.

There are a number of transsexuals and former transsexuals I interviewed who have very prominent careers. Some of those careers have been stymied while others have moved ahead, even though the persons have shifted their gender roles. I have the permission of these persons and all others I interviewed to tell their stories without using their real names. Common sense, however, tells me that even well disguised versions of their lives could provide enough information to cause problems in their lives. Suffice it to say I talked to persons who are so well-educated, have so much knowledge in their fields, and are held in such high esteem by their colleagues they were able to retain their positions throughout the gender congruity experience. It is one thing for companies to deal with persons in the lower echelons of the corporate structure who pursue gender congruity. It is quite another, however, to contend with persons who have so much education, knowledge, and prestige that they are virtually indispensable. That is why some large companies are taking the dilemma of transsexualism seriously and starting to search for alternatives to letting persons go. Some companies are establishing corporate policies regarding transsexualism, and when these policies are realistic and fair, they benefit other transsexuals who are not necessarily in positions of power. It is not uncommon, however, for some companies to make exceptions for valued employees rather than establishing precedents. Many companies feel it is beneath the corporate dignity to become involved with niggling matters such as bathroom policies in connection with transsexuals in transition stages. Other imaginative companies are finding ways of handling these problems, and the more prominent the transsexual employees are, the harder they try. On the face of it, this seems like much ado about nothing. Certainly a society which can find its way to the moon and back has the ability to find fair, discrete, and equitable ways of helping a very small percentage of individuals cope with personal dilemmas without destroying their careers and human dignity. We have become such a wasteful, throwaway society, it comes as a shock to learn we pay a price when we squander our natural resources. Although we are sometimes our own worst enemy, human beings — men and women — are our most precious natural resource. Just as we exact a toll on the quality of our life when we carelessly trash our environment, society pays dearly when we heedlessly toss about human lives as if they were empty, used up cans and bottles.

# Chapter 5
# CHILDHOOD
# THE INGENUOUS YEARS

When I was a young child, my parents had a summer home near the headwaters of a river in northern California. Our family ordinarily spent most of the summer there. Soon after school let out in June, we would pack up and head for the mountains. My father was not able to be there the entire summer, but he drove up from the San Francisco Bay area on weekends, then returned to his business endeavors during the week. Most summers he would arrange his affairs so he could spend a week or two with the family and commute back and forth the rest of the time.

Our summer home was a roomy, sort of put together as you go type of house located on a large shelf of land about eighty feet above the river. The slope down to the river was quite gentle, so it was only a matter of seconds for us to go down to the water from the house. Several hundred yards behind the house was a large, forested mountain; on the other side of the river was a mountain range.

A screened sleeping porch faced the river. I was the youngest child and always slept on the sleeping porch. To this day, I am not sure whether I slept there because I was the youngest and therefore had my choice, or because no one else wanted to sleep there, so I was relegated to the porch. Whichever way it was, I remember it was always cold at night, and I bundled up with my pajamas and lots of blankets and quilts. The most vivid memory I have of the sleeping porch was dawn. I usually awakened at the first light of day. Because we were between two mountain ranges in a river canyon, the sky was always light before the sun ever appeared. Down in the flatlands, as we summer mountain people called it, the sun made an appearance long before we ever saw it. The river was to the west of our home, so the sun always rose over the mountain range to the rear of the house. Since I was on the sleeping porch, I could not see the sun when it did appear. What I sleepily watched was the sunlight starting to bath the mountain across the river from me. Suddenly the

mountain top would glow in a spectrum of light. Slowly the

sunlight would creep down the mountain, tree by tree it seemed to me, until it finally reached the bottom, then inched its way across the river toward me. The sun, sweeping away the shadows on that mountain, was my very personal clock all summer long. I knew almost to the minute what time it was by checking to see how far down the mountain the sunlight had progressed. I virtually had the mountain's terrain memorized, and every tree, gully, or stump was as familiar to me as the location of different rooms in the house. This morning ritual was much more interesting to me than the things all of us as children do to while away the time. No avoiding the cracks or seams in sidewalks for me. I had a whole mountain and the sun to amuse me all summer! When the sun reached the river, I frequently fell asleep again, only to have my mom or dad interrupt that dreamland by announcing that breakfast was ready. Somehow, when we steal a few moments of extra sleep, it seems almost cruel to have the rituals of the day so rudely interrupt those precious moments.

Over the years the house underwent many changes. The sleeping porch no longer exists. The wall between it and the living room was taken down, and a large bay window overlooking the river was installed. This was a needed improvement, without question, but my little niche, where I could watch the sunlight tumble down that mountain, was gone forever. Later in life, when I had my own family, we also spent many pleasant weeks at that same summer home. By then, the living arrangements were quite changed; none of my children were able to have the same experience I had as a child. Two of my children, in the summer, did sleep on a sleeping porch in another house which was added to the property, but those porches did not face the river. I am sure, however, all my children have their own, very personal memories of times spent there. I could no more share those personal experiences with them than they could share with me the one I have described. Such experiences are the stuff that make up childhood memories, and they can never be the same from generation to generation. If I could wave my hand and restore that old house to its original design, my experience with the mountain and the sun would not be the same for me now that it was as a small child. If my father and mother were alive today and we could talk about that sleeping porch, their perceptions and memories of it would be quite different than mine were as a child.

In sharing this memory of my childhood with the reader, my intention is to illustrate how each of us is unique and how differently we all experience the same general set of circumstances. No doubt my brother and sister had their own, very personal memories of this summer home, quite different from mine. We all went swimming at the same places in the river, as did my children, but all of us came away from these common experiences with different perceptions and memories. Two things came to mind as I related this experience. Firstly, children experience life from quite a different perspective than adults do. Secondly, everyone experiences life in a very personal manner. Experiences in life are similar to snowflakes in the sense that no two are ever exactly alike. These fundamental realities were once again brought home to me when I asked transsexuals about their childhoods, the experiences they had, the feelings they felt, and how they reacted to those experiences and feelings. Their experiences and feelings were similar to the snowflakes: no two were quite the same, but they had much in common.

Carol told me about a dream she had when she was about four years old. That dream later became a fantasy for her. "I dreamed I was a princess who was just having a dream that I was a boy, and I would wake up and be a real girl. I became very confused and scared around puberty when I realized I wasn't going to be a girl. I knew I didn't feel like a boy, even though that was what I seemed to be turning into." Diane's feelings were similar but took a slightly different turn. "I remember praying I would wake up as a girl. My feelings caused me a lot of confusion, but I knew instinctively they were my deepest, darkest secrets, and I could never tell anyone. My mom used to freak out when she caught me cross dressing or playing with dolls. She would explain to me that this was considered effeminate behavior. I think mom accepted me for what I was, but was trying to warn me how the world viewed these things in order to protect me." Dan: "I was very confused and scared about my feelings when I was a kid. I didn't fit in with other girls even though I looked like one. It really confused me when people continually referred to me as a girl. When I reached puberty, I had a lot of anger and frustration about my situation. I didn't know what to do." Dorothy: "I can't ever remember not wanting to be a girl. I was very scared most of my childhood because of my feelings, and I cried about it an awful lot." Evelyn: "I can remember at about four I was dressing in girls' clothes, and sometimes my sister would dress me up. I just loved it. It is somewhat confused in my mind now, but I think I felt I was a girl, but something was really wrong. The reality that I wasn't a girl didn't really come home to me until I was twelve or thirteen. I remember being furious the first time I ejaculated, because that confirmed I really was a boy." Sam: "I remember, even before I started school, I preferred to wear clothes like my dad's, rather than like my mom's. In play activities I always liked to be in the male role. I liked to fantasize I would become a boy at puberty, even though I was aware of the realities." Eric: "I always felt I was really missing out on something. I didn't feel comfortable in any girls clothes. I wanted to be a boy and couldn't figure out why I wasn't one, though I knew I was a girl. I fought with my dad a lot about wearing girls' clothing. I was very confused about my feelings and why I wasn't a boy." Victoria: "I remember telling my mother I wanted to grow up to be like her, but she would just tell me I was going to grow up to be like my father. I was terribly confused about why I couldn't be a girl. My mother would call me a sissy when I expressed my feelings. That was very much of a put-down to me, and I felt my mother was right; I just didn't fit into the world." Roberta: "I used to get mad at my mother for calling me a boy. One time, when I was about four, I walked into the bathroom when my mother was taking a bath. I had my doll with me, and my mother said, 'Sissy, will you please put that doll down and start acting like a little boy'. I said, 'I'm not going to act like a little boy, 'cause I'm a girl'. My mother responded, 'You can't be a girl, 'cause you don't have this,' and she pointed to her vagina. I said, 'Mamma! What happened to yours?' "

Roberta was one of the least educated persons I interviewed; she was also one of the most intelligent. Although she did not have a large vocabulary, her language skills were amazing for someone with so little education. There is a richness and flavor to her speech one seldom hears. She told me how cruel her stepfather was to her. He used to insist on giving her a boxing lesson and forced her to drink liquor when she was a small child before he would let her go to the movies on Saturdays. He continually called her a fag in front of his friends and even took her to a prostitute when she was a teenager. He was determined to make a man out of her (at least his version of what constituted a man). When I first asked her what kind of man he was, she smiled and replied, "Honey, he was Archie Bunker in living color." Another time I asked her if she felt there was any relationship between transsexualism and homosexuality or transvestism. She looked at me with a straight face and responded, "Sure. They are about as closely related to each other as Winston Churchill was to a Zulu warrior."

Roberta was without question one of the most interesting persons I interviewed. She is a strikingly beautiful woman who carries herself with pride and dignity, yet she has been through so much. She was the first male-to-female transsexual to have surgery in the United States in 1965, and the problems she faced before and after surgery were monumental. Roberta has had a rough and tumble life, yet she is an immensely compassionate and religious person. When speaking of her ordeal, she said, "I mourn for transsexuals who came before me who were not able to do anything about their situations."

Transsexuals often lead lonely lives as children; they usually feel they are the only ones who experience the feelings they have, and they are afraid to talk to their parents or friends about their feelings out of fear of rejection or humiliation. They cross-dress in secret and develop deep seated feelings of guilt about their behavior. Eighty-four percent of the transsexuals I interviewed told me there had been one or more periods where they tried to purge their feelings and attempted to live life without cross-dressing and having feelings of wanting to be the opposite gender. Their efforts were spectacularly unsuccessful. Fern told me: "Many times I vowed that I wouldn't cross-dress anymore, but my feelings always came right back. I'd have the experience of sort of blanking out, and find myself dressed again." Kitty: "Many times I stopped cross dressing, but when I again had access to women's clothing I would go right back to it." Margaret: "We lived in the country on a ranch, and there were old, abandoned buildings all around the area that had discarded girls' clothes in them. I expended tremendous energy walking and running miles going to these buildings in order to dress in the clothes. I often vowed to stop doing it, but soon I would find myself right back at those old buildings." Eric: "I have been through many purges. I was even married to a man as a woman, and I made a real effort to get rid of my feelings at that time. I just couldn't do it." Susan: "I can't count the number of times I threw women's clothing, wigs, and makeup away, and vowed not to dress anymore or have the feelings of wanting to be a girl. But the feelings always returned and so did the female wardrobe."

The human race is the only animal species I know of which indulges in sexual activity for reasons other than procreation. In other animal forms of life, sexuality is cyclical, and sexual activity only takes place when the female is in that portion of her estrus cycle which is optimal for fertilization of her eggs by the male. She lets the male know when this time has arrived by a scent she may emit, her body language, or some other form of mutually understood communication. In some animals this only may happen once a year, while others may have cyclical sexual activity several times a year; but the sexual cycle always revolves around ovulation. Women ovulate and menstruate in their cycle which occurs every twenty-eight days. They ovulate in the middle of the cycle, as a rule, and only can be impregnated close to the time of ovulation. But the sexual interest of women and men does not correspond with ovulation as it does with other animals. While other species will indulge in sexual activity only at the time of ovulation, human beings enjoy sexual relationships throughout the female cycle. We are the only animal form of life to engage in sexual activity simply for the pleasures involved, as well as procreation.

Among the male–to–female transsexuals I interviewed, eighty-seven percent told me they had some form of sexual arousal when they dressed in female clothing, at least at some point in their lives. Others continued to have sexual stimulation until they started taking estrogenic hormones. The time of life this most often occurred was during the teenage years. Many behavioral scientists previously believed that if a genetic male had a history of sexual arousal from cross-dressing, that person was a fetishistic transvestite rather than a transsexual. A few people still hold this view, but most professionals who deal with transsexuals do not find this to be the case. My statistics certainly would seem to contradict any such theory. Some male–to–female transsexuals told me they had deliberately lied concerning this matter to therapists who were evaluating them for fear they would not receive a recommendation for surgery. Quite obviously they had no such motivation to lie to me.

The question of sexual arousal from cross dressing, on the surface, appears to be even more puzzling when we examine the statistics of the female–to–male transsexuals who answered this same question. Eighty–three percent of that group told me they had never been sexually aroused from cross-dressing. Now the plot thickens further. The seventeen percent of fe-

43

male-to-male transsexuals who told me they had become sexually aroused from cross-dressing all identified themselves as gay (one was not absolutely certain, but was pretty sure he was gay). In other words, they were genetic female-to-male transsexuals who wanted to become males, and identified with the gay male population. I will be discussing sexual preference as it relates to transsexuals, in Chapter 6, so let us leave that matter, for the moment, and concentrate on why most of the male-to-female transsexuals became sexually aroused from cross-dressing, yet most of the female-to-male transsexuals did not.

It would be difficult to prove scientifically why the dichotomy I have just described exists. Quite a bit of evidence does exist, however, which allows us to theorize. Some of the evidence is cultural in nature, and some is chemical-biological. Traditionally, women have been brought up in our society to be sexually passive. Until recently, women were not even thought to particularly enjoy sex. We know now, of course, that women can and do enjoy sexual relations. But women have been raised to play a passive role — the pursued, if you will, instead of the pursuer. Women traditionally have also been taught that sex is part of a loving experience and not something to be enjoyed outside of an intimate emotional and physical relationship — specifically, marriage. It is undeniable that the Madonna-whore syndrome has been a part of our social upbringing. Men have been raised to believe that sex, outside of an intimate relationship is perfectly acceptable, but women who indulged in casual sex were not the kind of women men were supposed to bring home to meet the family or marry. The women men married, in our society, were supposed to be chaste, and any woman who was not was considered to have loose morals. Women, therefore, were expected to be virgins at the time of marriage — unsullied, as it were, but enough of their promiscuous sisters were available to satisfy the lust of men. If men were not virgins at the alter of matrimony, they were considered experienced. If women were not virgins, they were harlots.

There were obviously some very good reasons these mores developed in society. In the early days of civilization, women had no control over when they might become pregnant, and that has remained true until very recently. Women, therefore, carried the responsibility of bearing and caring for children and were quite dependent upon men to provide food and shelter. Many of the customs which developed around these realities remained in place long after physical strength was no longer required to provide food and shelter, and women gained some control over their destinies due to the development of reliable contraception. This, of course, has led to a very sexist society. Women's liberation and the much heralded sexual revolution have made some inroads into the sexual traditions I have just described, but, in much of our society, the same values still prevail. As with all social mores, they change very slowly over many generations. In varying degrees, women in our culture have been raised to repress any sexual feelings they have, while men, by comparison, have had pretty much free rein over their sexuality.

The chemical-biological evidence I alluded to relates to the male hormone, testosterone. We all know that men produce testosterone in the testes, and women produce estrogen in their ovaries. What is perhaps not so well known is that men and women produce both of these hormones in very small amounts in their adrenal glands. These glands rest just above the kidneys. Various scientific studies have demonstrated that testosterone is the hormone which provides men and women with their libidos. Without this hormone in their systems, males and females both lose their interest in sex. It has also been successfully shown that when women have an abnormal amount of testosterone in their systems, their libidos increase. That is no doubt why two-thirds of the female-to male transsexuals who had been taking testosterone reported to me that their libidos had increased. The figure might have been even higher had I phrased the question differently. I simply asked what physical effects the hormone had upon them. I did not specifically ask about testosterone and their libidos. In some cases, the persons may have been more impressed with the fact that their voices had deepened or some other change had occurred and failed to mention anything about their sex drive. In a couple of instances, the individuals had only taken the hormones for a few weeks, so no noticable effects would have taken place.

Obviously men produce a great deal more testosterone than women. Scientists tell us that the peak years of testosterone production in males are the late teenage years. As a woman who considers herself a feminist and believes that many of the gender stereotypes we have are cultural in origin, it is difficult for me to reconcile those beliefs with the biological fact that men, at least in the early part of their lives, do seem to have higher sex drives than women. Nature appears to balance the picture out later in life, however. Women frequently do not reach their peak of sexual drive until they are older (the thirties and forties), while the sexual drive of men diminishes somewhat as they approach middle life. Certainly cultural elements play a part in this shift, but hormonal balances are key to these changes. In late adolescence, however, men do have more compelling sexual drives. Even crime figures seem to bear this fact out. Generally, men will go further and explore more avenues of sexual behavior than women will. Most of the sex crimes in our society are committed by relatively young men, not women. Pedophillia, for example, is an almost exclusive male interest as are any number of other bizarre sexual activities and crimes.

In view of the cultural and chemical-biological evidence, it seems clear to me why most male-to-female transsexuals might have become sexually aroused from wearing women's clothing, yet few of the female-to-male transsexuals did. It must be remembered that nearly all male-to-female transsexuals, prior to taking estrogen, have normal testosterone levels in their systems. It is also worth noting that thirteen percent of the male-to-female transsexuals I interviewed did not become aroused under similar circumstances. In almost all cases, those individuals, from the histories they related to me, appeared to have little or no sexual motivations throughout their lives. They virtually had no sexual relations, fantasies, or experiences in their adolescent or adult years, but even the male-to-female transsexuals who did become sexually aroused from cross-dressing indicated, by and large, sexual arousal just seemed to be part and parcel of cross-dressing — a side effect, if you will — not the real reason for cross-dressing. Most indicated that they cross-dressed because it helped to enhance their image of themselves in their fantasies as females. The majority of their fantasies revolved around being females, quite often in sexual situations with partners, but often just being females. Female-to-male transsexuals had the same motivations for cross-dressing, and their fantasies seemed pretty much the same. Sex, however, was not a part of their fantasies nearly so often as it was for male-to-female transsexuals. It seems difficult to interpret the statistical data I gathered in any other way in light of the cultural and chemical-biological facts I have been discussing.

The confusion many transsexuals have about their gender takes its toll on them as they pass through puberty and develop into sexual beings. Sexuality is an important aspect of gender, and when persons have gender discomfort, and often gender confusion, they are very likely to experience a great deal of confusion concerning their sexuality. Homosexuality, which is a sexual preference, transvestism, which is a sexual condition, and transsexualism, which is a gender condition, have all been linked together by the media and, all too often, by the gender community. Transvestism, transsexualism, and homosexuality are all minority conditions (if sexual preference can even be termed a condition). All, to some degree, involve sexuality, so a very loose bond has existed between transvestites, transsexuals, and homosexuals, even though their conditions and problems are quite different. They do have one common problem: they are all minorities in terms of sex or gender. I do not mean to imply that the homosexual community embraces transsexuals with open arms or that transsexuals enjoy the company and have much in common with transvestites and homosexuals. Far from it. Unless transsexuals happen to have homosexual orientations in their chosen gender roles, they have little in common with homosexuals or transvestities, but all of those groups suffer from public disapproval and, frequently, social ostracism. It might be assumed the commonality of social ostracism would provide a breeding ground for widespread acceptance of each other. That is far from the fact. As I point out in another chapter, transsexuals usually just want to live their lives as men and women and do not ordinarily want to be part of any particular group, life-style, or social cause.

Most of the transsexuals I interviewed who identified themselves as heterosexual in their chosen gender roles had often been confused about their sexuality at one time in their lives; they had explored the homosexual world and discovered there was no home for them there. Victoria put it this way: "When I was a teenager, I thought being gay was just to be very feminine. When gay guys behaved differently and acted like men, I thought they were ruining the best part of being gay. It took me a while to realize they were interested in men, not women. I thought, 'God! I don't even fit in here'." Carol: "About a year and one-half ago, I realized I had gone from identifying myself as a gay man to an effeminate gay male, I then realized I still wasn't getting at my true identity. Even in the gay world, though men would relate to me as a gay male, I always related to them as a woman." Eric: "When I investigated the lesbian world, I realized lesbians were relating to me as a woman, and I wanted them to relate to me as a man." Don: "I didn't find out about transsexualism until about two and one-half years ago when I was about thirty seven. I met a woman with whom I now live, and we became

47

very attracted to each other. We didn't feel the attraction was lesbian, like two women being attracted to each other. It was more like a man-woman relationship, so we were very puzzled and started reading different books. When I read an autobiography about a female–to–male transsexual, I understood our relationship, and the feelings I had all my life of wanting to be a man; not wanting to be a woman." Evelyn: "I looked into the gay world, but I always related to the men as a woman and, of course, they wanted to relate to me as a man." Pedro: "I just didn't know where I fit in the sexual world. I knew I wasn't a lesbian, because I just couldn't relate to women as a woman or be related to as a woman. I was afraid to approach straight women because of my biological characteristics."

Most transsexuals who explore the gay or lesbian worlds find they simply cannot relate to others of their biological gender in those roles. Some transsexuals will stay within the embrace of the gay or lesbian communities, because they can have relationships with persons they are attracted to even though those relationships leave much to be desired from the standpoint of transsexuals. Others will maintain their connections with the homosexual community, because they find some measure of acceptance there, unlike the rest of society. Most transsexuals who do explore the world of homosexuality, however, find it impossible to relate to members of their own gender in similar gender roles.

The most insightful point Roberta made was this remark: "If I had been born without an arm, the doctors would have done something about it and no one would have even thought twice. But since transsexualism can't be seen with the eyes (like a missing limb), people tend not to believe it."

Radio talk shows are a favorite pastime for me when I am doing things around my home which do not require a lot of concentration. Just this last week I heard a show about agoraphobia (a fear of being in crowds or open spaces, coming from the Greek word agora, which means marketplace). The guest was a woman who had suffered from this phobia for many years and finally had been able to find help. It is only recently that psychiatrists and psychologists have learned how to treat agoraphobia, and the guest was describing how she had been to numerous physicians, psychiatrists, and therapists who had not been able to help her. The physicians told her there was nothing wrong with her, although she was having acute physical symptoms of severe anxiety.

The therapists were at a complete loss as to how to help her. The woman described how frightening and confusing her feelings were to her. She felt as though she must be going crazy, because no one else seemed to feel the way she did or understand her feelings. Coincidently, a couple of days later I was listening to another talk show which was hosted by a psychiatrist. Listeners were calling the show to talk about children who had physical, developmental, and learning disabilities. One woman caller told about her son who had an acute learning disability which was not discovered until he was in the fourth grade. She said her son is now seventeen and has been able to talk to her about the terrible feelings of inadequacy he experienced during that early stage of his life and the internal frustrations he underwent. As I was listening to both of these shows, I was reminded of the interviews I conducted. The emotions of frustration, fright, and confusion expressed by the guest who had suffered from agoraphobia and the callers to the show about disabilities were almost identical to so many of the feelings related to me by transsexuals. The hosts of both shows and the listeners who called expressed warmth and understanding about the dilemmas these conditions caused. Had transsexualism been the subject of either of those shows, I wonder if there would have been as much understanding and warmth expressed and whether a good deal of skepticism might have been voiced. Somehow, when sex or gender enter the picture, this changes many persons' outlooks. Certainly the feelings transsexuals experience, usually from earliest memories, are just as disabeling as any other handicaps, whether they be learning disabilities, physical disabilities, or developmental disabilities. Society does not view transsexualism as a disability because, in large part, of the way it has been presented to the public. This is truly unfortunate, because transsexualism is devastating to the lives of those who experience it, and I do not think any transsexual or former transsexual would wish such an experience on anyone else. Here is how Carl described his feelings to me: "When I used to tell my mother I wanted to be a boy, she would just tell me I was a tomboy and would grow out of it. I didn't expect to grow out of my feelings, though I hoped I would. Life would have been so much more simple. I never wanted to be a girl, though *I wanted to want to be one.* The feelings of wanting to be a boy have always been with me, and they have underlined everything connected with my life."

Carl probably expressed the frustration as well as anyone when he talked about wanting to want to be a girl. The point is, of course, he could not have those feelings no matter how much he wanted to have them or however much he tried to have them. No one invites a guest of this nature into their lives. This condition we call transsexualism is nothing less than a very undesirable intruder. Transsexualism affects relationships with families and friends, retards social and career development, and creates tremendous burdens of guilt. I have talked to too many transsexuals and listened to too many sad stories to believe that transsexualism is anything but a very unwelcome guest, and an uninvited dilemma.

# Chapter 6
# ADULTHOOD
# THE RHYTHMS OF LIFE

## THE CONSTANT PRETENSE

This body of mine .. this physical shell,
Has brought more pain than words can tell.

What I am way deep inside, I have
always had to hide.

I've thrived on wishes and dreams,
And tried to supress the tears
and screams.

My time is consumed with this one
great hope
That until I can change, I'll be
able to cope.

But the game just keeps getting
harder to play,
Year by year, day by day.

The constant pretense brings much
sorrow,
Yet I try to cling to my hopes of
tomorrow.

For in tomorrow, I do see,
A whole new world through a whole
new me.

A great mistake occurred when I
entered this life,
For they call me a woman, and this
is my strife.

A man is what I was meant to be,
But in the mirror, that is not
what I see.

My will is bent as my illusions
shatter.
Being true to myself is all that
should matter.

They call me Jan, but I'm really
John,
And still the facade goes on and
on . . .

My strength to go on is often in
doubt,
But still I pray for a way out.

Will someone help me change this
body of mine?
So life will be more than
meaningless time?

Will I ever be able to make this
dream real?
Without guilt and worry of what my
family will feel?

I know not when my answer will
arrive,
So I stand on the edge, just
waiting to dive

To dive out of the void that is
me . . .
And become the man I should truly be!*

This poem was shown to me by Carl, the young man I spoke about in the preceeding chapter, at the time I interviewed him. I later asked him if he would allow me to use the poem in this book. It originally appeared in *The Phoenix Monthly-International,* a magazine which publishes articles, stories, poetry, news events, book reviews, and any other material that may be of interest to the gender community. I wanted to reprint the poem, because I feel it pretty much typifies the feelings many transsexuals told me they had as they left their childhood and adolescent years and entered adulthood.

As I write these lines, I am reminded of some words many of us used in our childhood days when playing hide-and-go-seek. "READY OR NOT, HERE I COME ." Ready or not is what happens to all of us as we enter the adult world, and many of us are ill-prepared to meet the challenges life

* Poem is reprinted by permission from the author of *The Constant Pretense,* published in *The Phoenix Monthly-International,* copyright April, 1981.

invokes on all of us. Judging from the information I gathered in my research, this is particularly true of transsexuals. Even though the men and women I interviewed had a high level of education, generally they were not doing well in careers. Many were struggling with problems of what to do with their lives much later in life than other young persons with comparable educational backgrounds. Equally perplexing social problems confront transsexuals as they become adults. However they may approach adult relationships, the problem of gender discomfort is always present, and it overlaps into their sexuality as well as most other aspects of their lives. On balance, the social, economic, and emotional problems adult transsexuals face are monumental. Most transsexuals grow up understanding little about their dilemmas and having a great deal of guilt about their feelings. Many try to involve themselves in society as though they did not have gender problems, only to find those problems continually thwarting their efforts. Gender discomfort seems to be a very rude intruder which has little regard for personal privacy. It manifests itself at inappropriate and unexpected times. Transsexuals, no matter how hard they may try, just cannot seem to elude the clutches of gender discomfort. Many transsexuals I interviewed fought their feelings for years. Some of them did this by getting married and having children. Others avoided any serious commitments. I did get the feeling, however, that many of the men and women I talked to, even if they may have postponed any action, felt, in varying degrees, the inevitability of where their feelings might eventually take them. Many, as Carl pointed out in his poem, realize they are living behind a facade.

Thirty percent of the female–to–male transsexuals I interviewed had been married to men at one time in their lives, and forty percent of the male-to-female group had been married to women at one point. Thirty–five percent of the female-to-male group had children, while twenty-four percent of the male-to-female group had children. One female-to-male transsexual had remarried as a male, and five of them had been married only as males. Three male-to-female transsexuals had only been married as females. If we keep in mind that the mean age of all the transsexuals I interviewed was just over thirty four, these statistics are quite important. Almost a third of all the men and women I interviewed had made serious attempts to live within the bounds of their genetic gender roles and involved themselves in the socially acceptable institution of marriage. Many of them became parents as well,      53 so they were, in the eyes of the world, able to function in their genetic gender roles for a period of time. Some would ask why they could not just have continued to function in these roles and not go through the process of gender congruity. This is a legitimate question and is probably best answered by the persons themselves.

Evette told me: "I was married to a woman for about three years, and we had two children. I just couldn't control the urge to cross-dress when we were married. About six years ago, my wife left me a note and told me flatly that if the cross-dressing were to continue, the marriage could not. She said I was a terrible sexual deviate. I packed my bags that same day and left. I haven't seen her, or the children since. I know she would never let me near my kids." Ivanie: "I was married to my wife for about three years; we are divorced now. Getting married was sort of a last ditch effort on my part to live in the male role. I just couldn't hack it." Jane: "I was married for twenty-six years, and we have three adult children. My former wife and I are on good terms, and I have pretty good adult relationships with my children. For the last several years, due to transsexualism, I felt I was going down hill pretty fast; I knew I was going to have to do something soon." Don: "I was married to a man for seventeen years, and we have four children. My former husband understands the frustrations I had of wanting to be a man when we were married and is quite supportive of what I am doing." Wanda: "I had a good marriage for eleven and one-half years. Fortunately, we didn't have any children. The pressure of my feelings of wanting to be a woman got so intense I had to get away and at least find out for myself if this was really what I wanted. My former wife has been trying to understand, but it is difficult for her to comprehend. She really was not aware of my feelings until I told her, so it came as quite a shock to her."

Many transsexuals have made real efforts to live their lives normally in their genetic gender roles. The answer to the question I posed earlier would seem to be: In many cases, the pressures of their feelings and the roles they are playing become too much for transsexuals. Some last longer than others, but most, sooner or later, find the constant pretense more than they can cope with emotionally.

The fabric of love, marriage, and adult relationships for transsexuals is terribly complicated. Many of the persons I interviewed who had been married or been in loving relationships with members of the opposite gender had truly been in love with their former mates. It seems that wanting to be a woman or wanting to be a man is not necessarily a deterrent to male-to-female transsexuals falling in love with women, or female-to-male transsexuals from falling in love with men. I did find this was a much more common experience for male to-female transsexuals, however. Several female-to-male transsexuals readily admitted to me they had not been in love with their husbands, and the marriage was more a matter of convenience than anything else. Female-to-male transsexuals can and do fall in love with men, however; male-to-female transsexuals can and do fall in love with women. Conversely, some transsexuals never have had relationships with persons of the opposite gender and have only had love affairs or been attracted to persons of their own biological gender. These contrasting experiences raise the issue of sexual preference as it relates to transsexuals.

Of all the facets of transsexualism I studied, none proved to be more complex than adult relationships and sexual preferences. There is layer after layer of complicated emotional factors, biological determinants, social mores, values, and judgments which often come together to create internal confusion and chaos. Feelings and preferences are not just black and white. I soon discovered I was dealing with a subject with so many subtle shadings, it was a little like trying to put together a jigsaw puzzle depicting a picture of a fog bank.

One of the questions I asked in the interviews was as follows: "If you wish to shift your gender role, what is your sexual preference in that role?" In the case of female to male transsexuals the results were pretty clear cut. Eighty percent of them told me they were heterosexually oriented in the male role; ten percent reported they were homosexually oriented, and ten percent were uncertain. I found it quite interesting that many of the female-to-male transsexuals who indicated they were heterosexual expressed feelings which could only be described as homophobic (a fear of homosexuality). I found these attitudes to be quite peculiar considering the minority condition transsexuals occupy. Interestingly enough, there was much less homophobia voiced by the male-to-female transsexual group. Quite the contrary. Only fifty-two percent of that group even identified themselves as heterosexual in their chosen gender roles. Thirty-four percent said they were bisexual, six percent said they were homosexual, and eight percent told me they really did not know what their sexual preferences were in the female role.

I asked another question which has an important bearing on this subject. "Have you had any experience, or do you have any way of judging whether you will be able to relate to the persons you want to relate to sexually in the opposite gender role?" Eighty-five percent of the female-to-male transsexuals answered "yes" to this question, while only fifty six percent of the male-to-female transsexuals said "yes." When I pursued this matter and asked for specific examples, I found that most of the female-to-male transsexuals based their answers on having had sexual relations with women in the male gender role. Many of the male-to-female group based their answers on internal, wholly subjective evaluations — beliefs, if you will — that they would be able to relate to persons they wanted to relate to sexually. In other words, many had not experimented in the female gender role and had not had relationships which were sexual in nature.

There are a number of possible explanations as to why male-to-female transsexuals seem to be less heterosexually oriented in their chosen gender roles than female-to-male transsexuals are. I certainly have no way of proving any theory, and I doubt that enough statistics are available at this time for anyone to come up with a solid, scientific answer. All I can do is present my personal impressions and let readers judge for themselves.

It is, on balance, a lot easier for women to put some distance between themselves and having to be feminine in our society. I have already pointed out that women can wear very androgynous clothing and receive little comment about their appearances. But males, in this society, generally come under much closer scrutiny concerning their masculinity than females do concerning their feminity. For a number of reasons, we seem to place a higher priority on manhood (as society defines it) than we do upon womanhood. It is generally true that many more unspoken (but nevertheless clear) expectations of being a "real man" apply in this society than is the case for women. The term "macho" for example, has no counterpart in reference to women. My personal observation is male-to-female transsexuals have more manhood to escape from than female-to-male transsexuals have womanhood to retreat from. Almost none of the female-to-male transsexuals I talked to had any negative remarks to make about men or women in any general sense; however, quite a few male-to female transsexuals expressed considerable hostility, dislike, and distrust of men in general. A large majority of those I interviewed seemed to agree that men, in many ways, were much more restricted in our society than women were, even though men may enjoy a little more status by virtue of their gender. Keeping these facts in mind, it would seem logical that many male-to-female transsexuals might well, at least for a period of time, want little to do with men on a social or sexual basis when they shift their gender roles to females. Perhaps they need a little time to be away from the male image they had been expected to live up to and they so thoroughly disliked. I followed this theory up, and in a number of instances male-to-female transsexuals identified themselves as bisexual or homosexual when they first shifted their gender roles, but a significant number seemed to lose their hostilities as they gained experience and confidence in the female role. They were able to be a little more objective and view men from a female point of view, rather than from the male perspective. Several male-to-female transsexuals, in the cross-living stage or after surgery, started to become interested in men emotionally and sexually, and some had decided they were not homosexual. Others who had identified themselves as bisexual appeared to be predominately interested in men as time went by.

No two situations are exactly alike, of course, as the fabric of adult human sexuality is intricately woven from innumerable strands of bio-chemical factors, genetic traits, and life experiences. The very complex interaction of the cultural, biological, and genetic phenomenon we all experience, and which I have been discussing, does lead me to believe these interactions may well be the root causes for the statistical variation I found in the male-to-female group with respect to sexual preference.

There is another issue concerning sexual preference as it relates to transsexuals which needs to be addressed. This issue concerns the fact that many transsexuals are attracted to persons of the opposite gender in their biological gender roles, yet find themselves attracted to persons of the opposite gender when they shift gender roles. In other words, many transsexuals who were born as genetic males may have been attracted to women until they pursued gender congruity. They then found themselves attracted to men when they started cross-living in the female gender role. This happens less frequently with female-to-male transsexuals, but it does happen in both groups. My interview was not designed to probe deeply into the sexual preferences of transsexuals, so I do not have any hard, statistical evidence to explain why such a phenomenon might occur. In this particular matter, I am relying on some of the insights I gained from interviewing and talking to a great many transsexuals.

Two factors may be involved in the phenomenon I have just mentioned. My interviews, without question, did establish the fact that most transsexuals do not, in fact, switch their sexual orientation when they shift their gender roles. Most remain heterosexually oriented. Of course this means they do shift their sexual interest from one gender to the other as they shift their own gender roles. Some persons advance the argument that transsexuals are really latent homosexuals, and they go through the process of gender congruity for the purpose of having sexual relationships with persons of their own biological gender. The persons who present such arguments believe that transsexuals, somehow in their own minds, are legitimatizing their homosexuality and using transsexualism as a guise. This is nonsense of the worst sort. If this were the case, why are some transsexuals homosexual in their new gender roles? Homosexuality is much more acceptable to society in general than it was just ten years ago. It is much easier for persons to acknowledge their homosexuality and find support from the homosexual community as well as support from a growing number of people in the heterosexual community. At the same time, more and more transsexuals are seeking help to resolve their problems through gender congruity. There is simply no need for homosexuals to take such a devious and dangerous path to achieve sexual peace of mind. Homosexuality or heterosexuality relates to sexual preference, but transsexualism covers the entire spectrum of human activities in the male or female gender roles. Transsexuals do not simply want to have sexual relations with persons of a particular gender. Sexual preference is limited to one area and one area only of human activity by its very definition. Transsexualism involves all aspects of living as defined by gender roles. Transsexuals want to relate and be related to by others as persons in gender roles different from those they were assigned at birth based on their sexual characteristics. Homosexuals have no such desires and only want to have sexual relationships with persons of their own biological gender.

Nature versus nurture, or biological determinism versus cultural determinism are areas which are continually debated and hotly disputed by various scientists. Frequently persons come down on one side or the other. Someone conducts a study which seems to prove that cultural factors are the reasons for specific modes of human behavior. Elaborate arguments then are constructed to affirm once and for all that cultural influence is really the dominant factor in influencing human behavior. A biological or genetic study soon follows which tends to indicate that genetic or biological factors are the reasons for some facet of human behavior. Again, arguments are constructed to sustain the theory that biological or genetic factors are the most critical elements which influence human behavior. Despite the fact that many scientists have come to realize human behavior is based on cultural, biological, and genetic components, it is surprising how many people still insist that one is more important or solely responsible for human conduct. Considering all of the scientific studies which have been conducted to examine human behavior, it should be obvious that we are the most complicated form of life ever to exist, and that our existence, life spans, and what we do on this earth are the products of extremely delicate balances of nature; they are based on where we came from, how we got here, how we are treated once we arrive, and how we react to what we find when we do get here. All of these ingredients work in harmony with each other, and this delicate balance we call human life can be profoundly influenced anywhere along the line.

I have no intention of involving myself in the debate, which seems endless, as to whether sexual orientation is caused by cultural factors or biological and/or genetic influences. Many who advance the theory that homosexuality is culturally determined use their positions to condemn homosexuality as something that can be changed; therefore, it does not deserve legitimate recognition. Keeping in mind what I have said about balancing factors and their influence on human behavior, I feel it is worth raising the question as to whether sexual preference may be a little more flexible than some feel it is and that it may have a relationship to gender roles, in some cases. This does not — and I emphasize *does not* — preclude the possibility that gender identity is influenced, if not determined in utero by various chemical-hormonal reactions. I will be discussing this possibility in a later chapter, but I raise the issue of flexibility here, because if gender identity is influenced by various chemical-hormonal events, whatever link there is between sexual preference and gender identity may well play a key role when transsexuals shift their gender roles but not their sexual preferences. The fact that some 59 transsexuals are homosexual in their gender roles of choice lends credence to the supposition that sexual orientation, at least for some transsexuals, is somewhat flexible and, perhaps, closely linked to gender roles. The non-transsexual population also has a statistical variation with respect to sexual preferences. What may be an important element here is that sexual orientation for some transsexuals may well be based more on gender roles than it is on biological determinants. Lest I be misunderstood, I am speaking here only about transsexuals and not the general population, and what I am proposing is supposition on my part. The fact is, however, that many transsexuals do shift their gender roles but not their sexual orientation. While it is true that the gender which sexually interests transsexuals shifts from male to female, or female to male, most transsexuals remain heterosexual within the context of the gender roles they are living. I am suggesting that in much the same manner as some persons tend to be monogamous while others are promiscuous, many transsexuals are heterosexually oriented, regardless of which gender role they may be fulfilling. Transsexuals I interviewed who had a history of sexual promiscuity in their genetic gender roles also tended to be promiscuous when they shifted their gender roles, regardless of their sexual orientation. Transsexuals who were monogamous in their original gender roles also tended to be monogamous after they shifted their gender roles, regardless of their sexual orientation. I submit that the same phenomenon holds true for transsexuals with respect to sexual orientation.

Let me tell you how Susan expressed her feelings about this matter and the experience she had. "I can't ever remember when I didn't want to be a girl and, as I grew up, to be a woman. I thought I must be sick or something, because I was truly sexually and emotionally attracted to women. They aroused me, and I enjoyed sexual relationships with them. What really confused me was the fact that even though women attracted me, my fantasies as a teenager and as an adult almost always revolved around my being a female. Even in actual sexual situations I usually fantasized I was a female being made love to by a male, although my partner was a female. I was married twice and very involved with another woman for a number of years before I first married. I have to honestly say I was very much in love with all three of those women, in every sense of the word. They were all long-term relationships, not just casual affairs.

"What really blows me away is that when I did start to cross-live, and then had surgery, I found I was no longer attracted to women sexually. I never thought twice about men sexually when I was in the male role, but now that I can look at men from the perspective of a woman, I find I am very much attracted to them sexually and in terms of emotional relationships. I find I still only want to be involved with one man, in the same way I only wanted to be involved with one woman when I was in the male role. The fact that this shift occurred so naturally has made me wonder just how much we really know about gender and sexuality."

Whatever causes the changes Susan noticed in herself and similar shifts I observed from interviewing others, the questions raised by them certainly deserve a long, hard look by a number of scientific disciplines. Answers to the questions raised by these issues, as suggested by Susan, might well provide us with a great deal more understanding of human sexuality and gender identity than we have at the present time.

When I first started my research to learn more about transsexualism, I took it for granted that when male to female transsexuals pursued gender congruity, they would only be interested in sexual relationships with men. Conversely, I thought that if female-to-male transsexuals shifted their gender roles, they would be exclusively interested in sexual relationships with women. It did not take me long to become disabused of that notion. When I first learned that some transsexuals had homosexual orientations in their chosen gender roles, I questioned whether they were really transsexuals at all and perhaps had sexual problems rather than gender discomfort. The question I asked myself was: Why would a man go to all the trouble to shift his gender role and then want to have lesbian relationships? Why not just stay a man, avoid all the problems involved, and have relationships with women as a man? This is a perfectly logical (although naive, upon reflection) question to ask, and it has been asked of me many times by friends who are familiar with this project. I explored this issue with several male-to-female transsexuals. I suspected there might be some political motivations behind male-to-female transsexuals who identified themselves as lesbians. Though many of them did have strong feminist orientations politically, this did not seem to be the reason they identified as lesbians.

For a large segment of the population, homosexuality is a difficult issue to cope with. To most persons, transsexualism is even more difficult to deal with; gender roles and gender identity are deeply fixed in people's minds. When these two conditions occur in one individual, the average person is tempted to throw up his hands in disbelief and walk away muttering and shaking his head. Not until I met a female-to-male transsexual who identified himself as a gay male did the dynamics of homosexuality in transsexuals become clear to me. I asked him the same question I had asked the others. If he was attracted to men, why not just remain a woman and have relationships with men? This man, Andy, pointed out to me that relating to men as a woman and relating to men as a homosexual male are two quite different life experiences. Of course when I looked at it in that light, the dynamics of such completely different experiences were obvious. What I was overlooking was the simple fact that homosexuality and transsexualism are two entirely different matters. Homosexuality is a sexual preference, and transsexualism is a gender condition. Both involve sexuality, of course, because we are all sexual creatures, but homosexuals prefer relationships with persons of their own gender. Heterosexuals, of course, prefer relationships with persons of the opposite gender. If a genetic male identifies as a female, there is no earthly reason to preclude such a person from having a homosexual orientation in the gender role she identifies with. If a female-to-male transsexual identifies as a male, again there is no reason to preclude such a person from having a homosexual orientation in the male gender role he identifies with. About ten percent of the population does have a homosexual orientation, and there is no reason to suppose transsexuals might be any different. If anything, the fact that some transsexuals are homosexual in chosen gender roles clearly indicates that homosexuality and transsexualism are entirely separate issues.

There is much controversy as to whether homosexual lifestyles differ from heterosexual lifestyles. Many homosexual couples do lead very close, monogamous lives, sometimes living an adult lifetime with one mate. Others contend that homosexuals lead very promiscuous lifestyles. That may be a little like the pot calling the kettle black in view of the tremendous increase we have seen in recent years of sexually transmitted diseases in the heterosexual population. Lifestyles and promiscuity, however, are really not germane to the concepts I am discussing. Whether homosexuals or heterosexuals lead more promiscuous lifestyles has precious little to do with whether persons are or are not transsexuals or homosexuals. The fact that homosexuals relate sexually to persons of their own gender and heterosexuals relate sexually to persons of the opposite gender is what is important. These are quite different experiences which have nothing to do with promiscuity or monogamy as comparative lifestyles. They are quite different orientations, and one cannot expect genetic females who identify as males to want to stay females and relate to males as females. They would be considered females and be related to as females under those circumstances. That is not the same thing as being related to as a man by other men and relating to other men as a man.

I want to take this discussion out of the realm of theory for a moment, and place it in the context of a life experience. Bill enrolls in college as a male. His life experience in college is from a male perspective. Now let us add another factor to the picture. Bill happens to be a male-to-female transsexual. He never has revealed his secret to anyone, and he is a reasonably attractive young man, women find him attractive and desirable. Now I am going to add one more dimension. Bill not only identifies internally as a female, but as a lesbian as well. He really desires to be a female, live life as a female, and experience life from that perspective. He also finds other women attractive within the context of his own female identity. Since Bill is identified to the rest of the college community as a male, there is no way Bill could experience college life as a female, let alone as a lesbian. Living life as a male and relating to women as a male is an entirely different experience from living life as a woman and relating to other women as a female. The male and female life experiences are quite different in our society, and the homosexual and heterosexual experiences of life are also not alike. That, of course, is exactly why a female-to-male transsexual who identifies as gay would not have the same sexual and life experiences with men, as a woman that she would have if she were to live life as a male. The same, of course, holds true for male-to-female transsexuals. Whether persons be heterosexual, homosexual, or bisexual, life in one gender role is quite different from that in the opposite gender role.

All the transsexuals I interviewed were asked the following hypothetical question: "Suppose, for some reason, you could not perform sexually in the opposite gender role. Would you still want to have the surgery?" Over ninety-four percent of the female-to-male transsexual group answered "yes" to this question. Eighty-one and one-half percent of the male-to-female transsexuals also responded "yes" to the same question. Not one person in the female-to-male group answered "no", and only one person in the male-to-female group said "no". All the rest who did not answer "yes" told me they were uncertain and would have to think the matter over. The overwhelming, positive response to this question has to be a clear indication that sexuality is not the motivating force behind transsexualism and the decision to pursue gender congruity. Most of those interviewed indicated they would not have been happy about such a condition arising, but the vast majority stated that they would still seek the surgery. Time after time, persons I interviewed told me that their personal images of themselves were the reasons they were pursuing gender congruity. Patricia put it this way: "Of course I would have been very disappointed if I had not been able to be sexually active as a woman, but living my life as a woman and being related to as a woman by others is what is most important to me. Actually, when you think about it, we spend much more of our life sleeping than we do having sex. But we live, relate, and are related to by others twenty-four hours a day as men or women. Sure sex is pleasurable, and I wouldn't give it up, but not being able to enjoy sexual relationships would not have deterred me from having gender surgery. It has added new meaning to my life, and I can live in a role I am comfortable with for the first time in my life. That is worth a great deal to me."

It has to be clear from Patricia's remarks and the responses I received to the question about sexual performance that sexual capability and pleasures are rather separate issues from gender roles and whether persons are comfortable in those roles. We are, as I have pointed out, all sexual by nature, and sexual activity is a very important aspect of our gender, but it really has nothing at all to do with the feelings of discomfort transsexuals experience in the gender roles they were assigned at birth. Sexual problems or sexual preferences are by-products of human beings as sexual persons, and they are sometimes compounded by gender discomfort. Gender discomfort can have profound effects on persons' sexuality, but sexuality, it would seem, has little effect on gender discomfort. Again, in my judgment, this is because sexuality is only one aspect of gender. Gender defines the total human being, while sexuality refers only to one specific aspect of that human being.

The answers to another hypothetical question I posed proved to be very revealing. The question was: "If you were told transsexualism could be eliminated from your life by psychotherapy, would you seek help?" Eighty-five percent of the female-to-male group answered "no" to this question, and eighty-eight percent of the male-to-female group responded "no". Again, the percentages are overwhelming. Carl, the young man who told me he wanted to want to be a girl as he was growing up but just could not have those feelings, also answered "no" to this question. On the surface, Carl's answer might seem to be in conflict with his earlier comments; in reality, it is not. Most transsexuals, as they are growing up, find their feelings to be frightening, confusing, and very uncomfortable. Few would wish to continue undergoing such wrenching emotions if something could be done about it. Most adult transsexuals who have acknowledged their situations, however, sometimes after years of denial, realize that nothing short of gender congruity will solve their dilemma. Most of the persons who answered "no" to this question told me they would not seek help, because for the first time in their lives they were comfortable with themselves and did not want to live their lives in any gender roles other than the ones they had chosen. Many felt such a change through some magical, non-existant psychotherapy would be to change the very essence of who they were; they just did not want to do that. This is, of course, an understandable attitude. If someone came up to you and me and told us he could make us not want to be the genders we were by means of psychotherapy, the stranger might quickly find himself on the way to the psychiatric ward of the local hospital. Even if things are not going well in our lives, none of us want to change our gender identity if we feel comfortable with it, and that surely is true for transsexuals who are pursuing gender congruity and most certainly for former transsexuals.

# Chapter 7
# THE OBSTACLE COURSE

Ordinarily, when we think of an obstacle course, we think of physical barriers: walls to scale, ropes to climb, hurdles to leap over, narrow spaces to crawl through, and many other barriers we all have seen. Transsexuals face quite another type of obstacle course. The barriers are of an entirely different nature. They test stamina and the ability to withstand physical pain to be sure, but most of all, they test psychological endurance, social acceptance, financial capabilities, willingness to submit to medical procedures, and emotional stability. Legal problems are usually present, business difficulties are everywhere, and rejection is readily available. If transsexuals decide to pursue gender congruity, there are myriads of questions those persons must find answers for, and there is little written material available to them which covers the broad spectrum of problems with which transsexuals have to cope. Specific answers can be found from various sources, but it takes a great deal of time and effort to come up with solutions to so many problems. If there is one glaring weakness in the transsexual process, it is the lack of information from readily accessible sources. Time and time again this complaint was voiced to me by those I interviewed and talked to. Some therapists have specific information which is of help to transsexuals, but most transsexuals, rightly I believe, resent having to pay money to therapists for this type of information. Therapy is very expensive, and the time should be spent working on emotional problems patients may have, not collecting practical information which should be available elsewhere at a much lower cost. In all fairness, this information void is not the fault of therapists, and sometimes it is necessary for them to spend valuable time providing practical information to transsexuals. This lack of information can cause real anxiety for transsexuals and, often, useful therapy cannot continue until individuals are able to solve pressing, day to day problems. On the other hand, some therapists possess little practical information, and transsexuals are left to their own devices to find solutions to their problems.

Legal matters can present very difficult problems for transsexuals. Laws vary from state to state, and individual judges may interpret the laws in quite different ways. Although we are a society of laws, the laws are made and interpreted by human beings. Judges, and juries for that matter, are human, and the way people see the law in rural areas, for example, is not necessarily the way others might see the same laws in an urban community. This is human nature, of course, and since we are such a diverse society, people are going to interpret laws in different ways. Though we sometimes complain about our cumbersome legal system — seemingly endless appeals, and the like — the system was formulated to insure a reasonable degree of egalitarianism in our diverse society.

Some state laws are reasonably sympathetic in providing transsexuals with humane protection, while other states have repressive laws, or, as in some states, no laws. No laws, in effect, grants authorities the right to discriminate against transsexuals. If, for example, a state refuses to change the gender of transsexuals on official documents, they will be subjected to ridicule in many cases and certainly denied rights all other citizens enjoy. Let me illustrate the difficulties faced by transsexuals or former transsexuals who are born or live in states which refuse to change the records of such persons. Frank was born and raised in a state which has no statutes relating to transsexuals and has no administrative regulations governing the treatment of transsexuals by public agencies. Frank moved to a state where help was available to him to resolve his gender difficulty. He pursued gender congruity, had genital surgery, and is now living life as a woman. Though Frank (now known as Fran) is presently living in a state which will recognize her change in gender identity, she would not be able to obtain a passport based on a birth certificate which reflects her new name and change in gender status. Fran would have to present evidence of a legal name change or proof that her new name is the one she has been using legally. In order for her passport to reflect her new gender status, she would have to furnish the Passport Division of the Department of State with a letter from her doctor. These same rules apply to pre-operative transsexuals. Prior to the late nineteen seventies, The Department of State would not issue passports without some proof of birth. Certainly their current policy is fair and realistic. States which refuse to issue revised birth certificates, however, put transsexuals and former transsexuals through the needless embarassment of presenting very personal information to a public agency; were it not for the realistic approach the Department of State has taken toward transsexuals and former transsexuals, many of them could not travel with a passport reflecting their current gender status. This type of neglect by some states is nothing more than de facto discrimination. By denying Fran recognition of her change in gender identity, her home state is subjecting her to public ridicule and humiliation by an act of omission. In my opinion, this is a violation of Section 1 of the Fourteenth Amendment of the Constitution of The United States which clearly says no state shall "deny to any person within its jurisdiction the equal protection of the laws". This clause does not say "any person *except*". It says unequivocally "*any person*", and that means any and all, not just those for whom states choose to provide such protection. Certainly Fran's right to privacy is being violated. Should she move back to her home state and request that a driver's license be issued in her new identity, that request would be denied unless she did not reveal her past. In other words, in order to attain equality, Fran would be forced to lie. Again, Fran would be discriminated against through legislative omission and not allowed to lawfully enjoy priviliges other qualified residents of her state enjoy.

Fran's problems reflect on just two areas where the law can have serious effects on the lives of transsexuals and former transsexuals. Though common law generally allows persons to use any name they so desire, so long as it is not for the purpose of perpetrating a crime, some states will not grant legal change of name to persons who have undergone gender congruity surgery. Even affidavits from surgeons stating that they have surgically changed the genital characteristics of persons from male to female or female to male will not help those individuals in states which refuse to recognize such changes under the law. This lack of recognition of change in gender identity can obviously cause serious and continuing problems for transsexuals. Real property ownership, personal property ownership, inheritance, and numerous other legal matters which arise in all of our lives can be affected; if nothing else, this statutory neglect can cause transsexuals to face continual legal problems and the expectation of life-long invasion of privacy far beyond what other citizens are forced to endure in our society.

Perhaps the most serious, and certainly one of the more cruel, legal problems which sometimes arises for transsexuals is in the area of criminal justice. Transsexuals who become enmeshed in the criminal justice system in this country (particularly transsexuals in a transition stage) frequently face total humiliation and, often, life-threatening situations. Many jurisdictions are totally unwilling to recognize the fact that transsexuals face very special problems if they are incarcerated. When transsexuals, be they male-to-female or female-to-male, are taken into custody, they are subjected to continual sexual harassment, regardless of whether they are lodged in female or male quarters. I interviewed two transsexuals who had been arrested, and the guards in charge of their custody had encouraged other prisoners to attack them sexually. In one case, the transsexual was molested by one of the guards. Sexual harassment of prison inmates is a well documented, rampant problem in this country. Transsexuals, by the very nature of their situations, have very special problems when incarcerated, and they deserve to be protected, regardless of the crimes they may have committed. Some courts are beginning to recognize these special problems, and are ordering prison officials to provide special facilities while housing transsexuals charged or convicted of crimes. The San Francisco Chronicle, on Saturday, April 16, 1983, carried a story describing just such a situation. A United States District Court Judge granted a preliminary injunction, which has since been made permanent, to a pre-operative, male-to-female transsexual convicted of bank robbery. The judge ruled that she was not to be housed in the male population of any prison, because he agreed with the petitioner that to do so could pose a real danger to her life. The judge also ruled that the petitioner would not have to be housed in the general population of a woman's prison either, because she would be subjected to physical abuse by lesbians. The judge recommended the prisoner be kept in an administrative segregation unit in a hospital setting where she could continue her hormone treatments. He ordered the treatments to continue, because the inmate could have severe psychological trauma should they be stopped. The article goes on to note that prison officials had classified the petitioner as a man, because genital surgery had not yet been performed. The judge stated the evidence "is overwhelming in every respect" that the prisoner has predominantly female characteristics, and "is a true transsexual."

Just as is the case with the general population, some transsexuals do commit crimes, and certainly they should pay the price when they do so, but that does not mean their basic human rights should be disregarded simply because they are transsexuals. Prison officials provide special care for other prisoners who might face life-threatening situations if they were to be housed with general prison populations, and no less should be done for transsexual prisoners.

Another cruel legal dilemma which some transsexuals have to face is the question of child custody or visitation rights for transsexual parents. If a former spouse of a transsexual parent becomes angry or hostile toward a transsexual parent, the transsexual may be forced to give up any relationships with his or her children or try to fight for his or her rights in a court of law. Most transsexuals are reluctant to draw attention to their situations by engaging in open confrontation. Former spouses of transsexuals really have an unfair advantage in these situations, because if transsexual parents should elect to fight for their rights, they would expose their dilemmas to the whole world and, in most cases, they would not be fighting legal battles on their own merits; they would be confronting societal disapproval of their conditions. Many persons have strong moral prejudices against persons who happen to be transsexuals. The question of whether individual transsexual parents are fit parents and should or should not be allowed to continue relationships with their children all too often become secondary, lost issues. Being a fit parent has nothing to do with whether someone is a transsexual. A fit parent relates to whether someone will take proper care of the children and provide a healthy environment in which the children can have reasonably secure relationships with the parent, be the parent male or female. It well may be some transsexual parents are indeed not fit parents, but that determination should be made on the basis it is decided in other cases — the general welfare of the child — not whether the parent happens to be a transsexual. Some transsexuals I met probably would not make fit parents. On the other hand, I have met many people in the world who would not, in my judgment, make fit parents. Conversely, many transsexuals I met have the ability to provide a warm, loving, secure, and intellectually stimulating atmosphere for young children. Transsexualism should not be the issue when a decision is made regarding fitness. As I see it, that is a totally extraneous issue, and discrimination again rears its ugly head.

Since laws very radically from state to state — if they exist at all — regarding transsexualism, transsexuals who face legal problems should obtain as much information as possible about their particular problems. J2CP Information Services, P.O. Box 154, San Juan Capistrano, CA 92693-0154, publishes a booklet which addresses itself to transsexuals and the law. The Southern California Chapter of the American Civil Liberties Union in Los Angeles, California, has a recently formed Transsexual Rights Committee. Any transsexual who encounters legal difficulties would be well-advised to contact either one or both of these organizations.

In addition to legal problems, business matters can often pose threats to the privacy of transsexuals as well as creating serious roadblocks to earning a living. The majority of institutions will handle changes of names in a routine manner. Most changes are the result of women getting married or divorced. These requests, as a rule, are dealt with routinely, and no further information is requested. Transsexuals, however, usually are changing their given names and, in some instances, their surnames. The given name is usually being changed from one considered masculine to one thought of as feminine, or one considered feminine to one thought of as masculine. These types of changes often call attention to the changes by employees at the businesses or institutions which are being requested to make those changes. If this happens, they are likely to ask for proof of the name change. Most transsexuals do not have their names legally changed, if they do so at all, until after they have had genital surgery, although there are exceptions. States which do recognize changes in gender identity and issue revised birth certificates require affidavits from qualified surgeons before they will make those changes. If pre-operative transsexuals do receive requests for proof of name changes, it is wise for them not to become hostile and demand their rights. Frequently, polite letters to the businesses or institutions, pointing out that it is legal for them to use any name they wish, providing it is not for the purpose of perpetrating a crime, will bring about positive results. If resistance is still met, it can be quite helpful for them to have attorneys write letters explaining the law. This almost always brings the desired results, but there are, of course, exceptions. If companies are being requested to make these changes, it should be kept in mind that most companies want more business, not less. Businesses are competitive, and transsexuals need to remember that they have the option of doing business with other companies. If credit ratings are involved, no company has the right to turn in negative credit ratings on persons just because they have requested that a company change their records.

Institutions such as government bureaucracies, labor unions, and the like are not competitive. Universities are an exception to that rule, but the effect is the same if transsexuals have attended particular universities which hold their records. Attitudes of government bureaucracies will vary according to state laws, or lack therof. California, and some other states, for example, recognize that one of the requirements for treatment of gender dysphoria is for persons to cross-role live for a period of time prior to surgery. This would prove to be very difficult without proper identification, because we live in a society which functions on the basis of identification cards, credit cards, and electronic access cards. California and some other states which recognize the dilemma of cross-role living, will change the names and gender identifications on driver's licenses, if individuals provide letters from physicians or qualified therapists indicating that they are being treated for gender dysphoria. Many states will not do this, and transsexuals are faced with the prospect of perhaps moving to an area where they can receive proper documentation. Such moves might require persons to interrupt their education, leave loved ones, or place themselves in financial jeopardy by quitting their jobs. These are not pleasant circumstances to face, and they are only a few of the obstacles many transsexuals must overcome along a very treacherous path.

Some institutions, like universities, are quite willing to comply with change of name requests, and most transcripts do not have gender identification on them. On the other hand, some universities and other institutions are quite adamant about requiring legal proof of name change, and in some cases transsexuals are forced to wait until this can be accomplished. In the case of Social Security records, there seems to be no problem. The Social Security Administration has a change of name form. All that needs to be done is to fill the form out, take it to a local office, and show some identification with one's new name and an old Social Security card showing that person's previous name.

There are no hard and fast rules governing all the situations I have been discussing, but transsexuals who decide to try the test of cross-living should be prepared to experience some resistance on the part of some companies and some institutions. Based on the experiences of all the transsexuals I interviewed and talked to, they would be well advised to realize society is not always going to be fair to them, and they are going to experience a certain amount of discrimination. If they are prepared for these eventualities, they may be somewhat less upsetting. Their efforts, however, are best directed at achieving their ultimate goals, rather than using up their energies engaging in continual skirmishes with elusive and nebulous enemies. Many other problems lie ahead for them which will require all the energy they can focus.

Employment and financial affairs frequently are troublesome areas for many transsexuals. Many young transsexuals who have no training and limited education find it difficult to enter the job market. Surgery for transsexuals is very expensive, and persons with little or no work background and no training or higher education would be wise to seek help from professional job counselors. Of course this advice would apply to any young people who find themselves in similar circumstances. Some states, through their departments of employment, have trained personnel to help persons prepare themselves for various careers. By testing, they can help individuals determine what types of skills they have and what their areas of interest are. They also can direct individuals to various training programs to help prepare them for careers.

Some transsexuals who have established careers sometimes find themselves in situations similar to those with little work background. They may be in jobs they do not wish to continue in after they start to cross-live or which are strongly associated with their biological gender. If this is the case, they also will have to seek out job counseling and consider learning new skills.

Some transsexuals find themselves with careers they enjoy, careers they chose out of personal interest and which they may have spent years preparing for. These persons probably do not wish to give up their careers, but it is usually awkward to try and remain with the same firm or institution after shifting gender roles. Good references to find similar employment with other firms often then become a problem.

Transsexuals are usually reluctant to approach supervisors or employers for references, because they are embarassed to reveal their situations to them, or they are afraid of being turned down and humiliated. These are genuine and understandable fears. Rejection is the most difficult emotion any of us ever deals with. We have all experienced it in our lives, and most of us will go out of our way not to expose ourselves to it. The fact of the matter is, however, if persons are good employees, employers or supervisors will usually accommodate them and give them good references. Employees who do inferior work, have poor work habits, or hostile attitudes will usually get negative responses.

Many employers who value transsexuals as employees will even try to keep them, in some instances. This may work in some cases, but usually other employees in the companies become a problem. Sometimes large companies with branches in many cities will transfer transsexuals, and it is then possible for them to get fresh starts with new people and not sacrifice knowledge, seniority, and skills in the process.

One area of treatment for male-to-female transsexuals deserves a special comment. I refer to electrolysis (the permanent removal of hair through the use of electric current, heat, or both). When testosterone is secreted in the male at puberty, it affects facial and body hair growth patterns, as well as the vocal cords. Many male-to-female transsexuals have normal beards and sometimes extensive body hair. Since we live in a culture which deplores facial or body hair on women, most male-to-female transsexuals need to undergo extensive electrolysis to remove normal beards and, in some cases, body hair. This treatment is quite painful, and the expenses are enormous. Many transsexuals need to have several hours of treatment per week, sometimes for two and three years. Most electrologists charge very high fees, and few of them are worth what they charge. Susan spent over nine thousand dollars in one year on electrolysis. After a year, she let her beard grow. She discovered, much to her chagrin, that her beard was just about as thick and tough as when she started treatment. She went to another electrologist, and within a year and one-half her beard was gone; this time she only spent about forty-five hundred dollars. I use the word "only" in a relative sense, because forty-five hundred dollars is a great deal of money. Many transsexuals get taken by electrologists, and transsexuals would be well advised to thoroughly investigate operators before going to them. Another young woman I interviewed, Ida, had spent over nineteen thousand dollars; and she still was receiving treatment! The success of electrolysis seems to be quite dependent upon the skill of individual operators and the methods they use. Additionally, incompetent operators can cause permanent skin damage at very high fees, and the kinds of sums I have mentioned are simply unconscionable.

Surgery for transsexuals is becoming more and more costly as medical costs go up. Electrolysis for male to female transsexuals can be very costly, as I have indicated. Many transsexuals have children for whom they are financially responsible, and these obligations should be met above all else. Transsexuals also have to take into consideration whether they will have money to live on after undergoing surgery. It takes time to heal, and they will not be able to work effectively immediately following surgery. All these matters require serious financial planning on the part of transsexuals.

All transsexuals face the problem of appropriate grooming, appearance, and mannerisms when they decide to cross live. No one has the right to tell another how he or she should appear in public with respect to grooming and style of dress. It is a fact of life, however, that society does make judgments concerning appearance, and there are certain generally accepted norms as to what is presentable for men and women. It would seem realistic, if transsexuals want to be accepted by society in opposite gender roles, that they certainly would increase those possibilities by making efforts to learn some of the basic grooming habits and behavior patterns of others in those roles. Although transsexuals may have wanted to be in opposite gender roles most of their lives, that does not necessarily mean that they will know how to groom themselves or present themselves in conformity with those gender roles. Things like dress, cosmetics (in the case of male-to-female transsexuals), body language, speech mannerisms, and numerous other very subtle behavior patterns are learned by boys and girls over a long socialization process in their assigned gender roles. Girls, for example, are usually not brought up to be as assertive as boys are, and some female-to male transsexuals may need some training to become more assertive. As I point out in Chapter 8, estrogenic hormones will not alter voice pitch or speech patterns. Many male-to female transsexuals need professional help from Speech and Language Pathologists in order to be able to use their voices in ways which do not identify them as male, despite their appearances. Abbey, a former male-to-female transsexual I interviewed, suggested it would be a good idea if there were some sort of half-way houses for transsexuals who are in transition so they could learn some of the things I have been discussing. That, as opposed to going out into the world cold in cross-living situations. I would have to endorse such a concept in general, as it certainly would help to reduce some of the initial awkwardness and fears most transsexuals have when they first approach the cross-living experience; many persons I interviewed expressed these fears.

Probably the most serious obstacles most transsexuals have to overcome are not necessarily of a practical nature, like the ones I have been discussing. The obstacles I refer to are emotional in nature, and they often create serious roadblocks to gender congruity. I pointed out in Chapter 2 that transsexualism is not necessarily an emotional illness as such, but that it could cause serious emotional problems for those persons who have such a condition. The feelings transsexuals experience can create fear, panic, anger, confusion, self-loathing, guilt, paranoia, and many other feelings detrimental to emotional well-being. In addition, if transsexuals reveal their feelings to others, they often experience rejection, and that can be one of the most destructive experiences human beings undergo. We all remember as girls and boys wondering if the boy we liked would ask us to the dance, or if the girl we wanted to ask to the dance would say no. These are childhood rejections we all experience to some extent, and most of us learn to cope with them and maintain a balanced view of life; certainly none of us enjoyed the experiences, although we probably learned from them. Transsexuals quite often endure a much harsher form of rejection: they frequently are rejected by society as a whole and their loved ones as well. These are devastating rejections to most transsexuals, and can lead to serious emotional dysfunction. All transsexuals, ultimately, are faced with the problem of telling family and friends about their situations. For most, this becomes a highly charged emotional issue. Transsexuals are opening the door to rejection when they reveal their feelings to others, and we all dread such a possibility. My research revealed that there is no simple answer to the problem, and no magic formula. The issues must be faced sooner or later, and no situation is exactly the same. Some families and friends may reject transsexuals out of hand initially and over a period of time find ways to accept them in part or in whole. Some families and friends may reject transsexuals completely and never have anything to do with them again. I cannot think of a more crucial emotional period for transsexuals. If ever there was a time to seek professional help to deal with problems and get some support, one has to think this is it. Based on the information I gathered, there is going to be some rejection for most; qualified therapists can be of tremendous help in learning to cope with rejection.

For some transsexuals, age becomes an issue as to whether they should pursue gender congruity. We live at a time where great emphasis is placed upon youth and beauty. I think this, in part, may explain why some transsexuals feel it is too late in life for them to shift their gender identity. Some feel this at thirty and some at fifty.

In years past, there were extended families and a constant mix of the old and young in many aspects of life. In our modern culture, we have separated the young from the old, in many cases. Grandparents seldom live with their children and grandchildren anymore. Instead, we have built retirement communities and retirement homes. The socialization process has been thrown off balance. No longer do we have a mixture where age is balanced with the vigor and vitality of the young and youthful enthusiasm is tempered with the wisdom of age. We have become a culture which only values the young. This is where the earning power is, and that is what we concentrate on. Older people, all too often, are conditioned to devalue themselves, accept their passive roles, and drop out of life at a time when they may have the most to contribute. Patricia expressed it this way: "I felt emotionally disabled prior to shifting my gender identity, and yet today I have never felt more alive and eager to face the future. Though I was fifty-two when I had gender reassignment surgery, I look forward to many years of participating in life as a person comfortable with her gender identity for the first time."

So much emphasis is placed upon youth and beauty these days, we tend to forget we all have intrinsic value as human beings. The middle and even the later years of our lives can be the most rewarding of all. Many of the pressures and responsibilities we faced when young have passed on. We can look at life through years of experience, and that experience can help us sort out the important and valuable things in life. Experience does not guarantee wisdom, but it certainly grants us the opportunity to view life with some realistic perspectives and learn to appreciate what we do have in this world.

Most of us grow up with "hangups" of one sort or another. We all, at one time or another in our lives, are wise if we seek help in dealing with problems not easily coped with by ourselves. It is difficult to be objective about ourselves, particularly at times of emotional stress. Many people just muddle through these periods, while others seek help, clear the air, and learn to deal realistically with their problems. A happier, more fulfilling life is usually the result.

Transsexuals face unique problems in this respect. They also grow up with "hangups" which are not necessarily related to their problems of gender identity. Emotional crises can be compounded for transsexuals, because they are dealing with the normal complications of life as well as identity problems. Transsexuals grow up, go to school, have relationships, sometimes get married, sometimes have children, earn their livings, and go through all the normal life processes of a modern society. As I have indicated several times, changing gender identity is a long and difficult process. There are many unusual emotional problems to cope with, and they drain one's emotional strength and energy. The process is taxing to the limit, and if transsexuals have not learned to deal with aspects of their emotional lives other than gender identity, they tend to overburden their emotional capabilities. I cannot stress the last point too strongly. Based on the problems that transsexuals have told me they encountered, I would have to recommend without reservation that all transsexuals get their emotional houses in order before attempting to shift their gender identities. It will take all their time and energies, and if they try to deal with that as well as extraneous emotional difficulties at the same time, an emotional collapse is quite likely to result.

Let me illustrate what I am saying. If someone is still blaming one or both of his or her parents or some other third party for causing some problem in his or her adult life, how in the world is that person going to establish an independent identity in another gender role? One thing is certain: if transsexuals are neurotic prior to genital surgery, they will be neurotic after the surgery. Genital surgery does not create mental health, nor is it any kind of cure-all for emotional problems. It is fraught with its own traumatic results. It does not even make individuals men or women. It provides them with the sexual characteristics of men or women; the rest is up to them. There is no magic to surgery. It simply gives transsexuals the opportunity to live comfortably in specific gender roles. It furnishes them with the tools, as it were. It does not teach them how to use them.

What I am trying to stress is this: emotional stability is so very important to transsexuals when they undertake shifting gender identity. It requires determination, singlemindedness, patience, and an ability to deal with emotional issues far more complicated than ordinary people ever face. That is why it is so important for transsexuals to clear the debris from their emotional attics if they want to be successful in their efforts, and live happy, useful, and productive lives. Professional people who work with transsexuals realize the difficulties which lie ahead, but they are not always listened to by transsexuals eager "to get on with it." I hope that this word of caution, based on the experiences of the many transsexuals I talked to, will lend credibility to the very real concerns those professionals have for the welfare of transsexuals.

# Chapter 8
# MEDICAL ARTS AND CRAFTS

Ever since 1952, when banner headlines proclaimed MAN BECOMES WOMAN, in reference to Christine Jorgensen, modern medicine and surgery have played a critical role in the lives of transsexuals. Many physicians and therapists have become specialists in helping and treating transsexuals. A number of gender clinics exist throughout the United States, and a kind of symbiotic triad exists between physicians, transsexuals, and therapists. These specialists and gender clinics would have to find other endeavors were it not for transsexuals, and transsexuals could not pursue gender congruity were it not for the skills of the specialists and gender clinics. Nowhere is the triad better exemplified than in the gender clinic. Here, transsexuals can be evaluated medically and psychologically. They can be provided with hormone therapy, psychotherapy and, eventually, surgery. The gender clinics are usually associated with major universities and offer the sort of enclosed mall concept which has become so popular in suburban shopping areas. Everything is offered under one roof with a controlled atmosphere thrown in. Transsexuals who do not live close to gender clinics or do not wish to move to areas which have gender clinics must rely on individual physicians and therapists for assistance and arrange independent surgical intervention.

Historical reflection seems to indicate that transsexualism has existed in many cultures throughout history, but, until the middle of this century, the medical community could offer little aid or comfort to the plight of transsexuals. As physicians gained knowledge of the endocrine system and the functions various hormones perform in the human body, modern surgical techniques were keeping pace. When hormonal and surgical intervention became a reality, the behavioral scientists assumed a natural role in helping transsexuals cope with behavioral and emotional problems which are frequently concomitant with the condition of transsexualism. In making this last statement, I must refer back to my comments in

Chapter 2 and again emphasize that behavioral and emotional problems frequently are the result of the transsexual condition. In no way do I mean to imply that emotional problems cause transsexualism. Conversely, emotional problems often do cause gender confusion, and that confusion, in turn, can lead persons down very false trails. True gender discomfort can only be ascertained after any gender confusion has been explored and resolved. Gender congruity is a solution for a very small percentage of persons who have gender confusion, and even then it is a treacherous path, strewn with hidden obstacles. It is a veritable psychological mine field and should be approached with some trepidation and great caution. Few cross from one side to the other without sustaining serious injuries.

In 1953, Harry Benjamin, M.D., a New York city endocrinologist, introduced the term "transsexual" to the medical community. Dr. Benjamin is considered by most persons to be the father of transsexualism. There is now the Harry Benjamin International Gender Dysphoria Association, Inc. to which most professionals who provide services for transsexuals belong. That association has adopted a standards of care statement relative to transsexuals. The Standards of Care statement has many sections, and I shall not go into them in detail. Its basic purpose is to provide minimum guidelines for professionals who treat transsexuals. The most important provisions of this document, from the point of view of transsexuals, relate to hormonal, psychological, and surgical care of transsexuals. For example, the standards require that hormone therapy only be given upon the recommendation of a behavioral scientist who has professional experience working with transsexuals. The psychiatrist or psychologist recommending hormone therapy must know the patient in a psychotherapeutic relationship for at least three months before such a recommendation can be made. The physician who administers hormone therapy must warn the patient of the possible consequences of receiving hormones, and that physician should exercise care in monitoring the patient while hormone therapy is in progress. The person must cross-live at least one year prior to receiving a recommendation for surgery, and that person must be observed for at least six months during the cross–living period by the professional making the primary recommendation for surgical intervention. Additionally, peer review is mandatory. If a psychiatrist makes a surgical recommendation, it is required that another, independent recommendation be made by some other behavioral scientist. If a psychologist makes a surgical recommendation, another, independent recommendation must be made by a psychiatrist. Numerous topics are covered in the Standards of Care statement, and I have only tried to cover some of the highlights.

It must be remembered that the standards of care I have been discussing are only minimum guidelines and, to my knowledge, carry no force of law. Many physicians who have had extensive experience in treating transsexuals can and do prescribe hormone therapy independent of any recommendations by psychologists or psychiatrists. Some of these physicians are probably better qualified to judge whether persons are good candidates for gender congruity than many behavioral scientists. There are, however, incompetent and unscrupulous people in all professions, and the medical profession is not an exception. Some doctors will prescribe hormones for anyone who asks for them and collect a fee. Some do not even perform or prescribe simple tests to determine the condition of persons receiving hormones.

In the animal and human world there are two types of sexual characteristics: primary and secondary. The primary sexual characteristics, in both the animal and human world, are the reproductive organs of males and females. Secondary sexual characteristics differ remarkably in the animal world, very much unlike human beings. The male lion's mane, for example, is his secondary sexual characteristic; so too is the iridescent plume of the male peacock. Secondary sexual characteristics are, on balance, quite uniform in human beings. There are some subtle racial differences, to be sure, but they are minor indeed. Generally speaking, males at the time of puberty start to develop beard and body hair growth patterns not usually found in females. The vocal cords of males start to thicken and elongate, giving them deeper voices than females. Males frequently become subject to male pattern baldness, if those genes are passed along by their mothers. Males, as a rule, usually have less fat per pound of body weight than do females and are much more prone to muscular development than females, particularly in terms of upper body strength.

Women, on the other hand, go through their own changes at the time of puberty. The most notable secondary sexual characteristic of females is the development of breasts. Women do not experience growth of the vocal cords, and their voices do not undergo sudden changes. The distribution of fatty tissue takes on a different pattern for women than it does for men, and women usually have a wider spread to their pelvis. Most women do not develop much beard or body hair, and their skin is usually less porous and smoother. This sometimes changes after menopause, and it is not uncommon for many women to develop some facial hair growth at this stage of their lives due to lower levels of estrogen in their systems.

Androgenic (i.e., testosterone) and estrogenic (i.e., estrogen) hormones (also known as sex hormones) are very powerful drugs which can have profound effects on the human body. Some of the effects may be desirable for transsexuals but some of the side effects may not. Both of these hormones, for example, can elevate blood pressure, increase triglycerides (fatty acids) in the blood, and stress the liver. The liver metabolizes sex hormones, and excessive dosages of them can greatly overtax the liver and cause serious damage. In addition to physiological problems, sex hormones can cause serious emotional distress. Pat, a male-to-female transsexual I interviewed, has been taking estrogenic hormones for over five years. When she takes the normal amount prescribed for pre-operative transsexuals, she experiences acute depression and sudden, violent mood swings. Pat has only been able to take very small amounts of estrogen, and these dosages have not been sufficient to help her develop any secondary female sexual characteristics. This is a very real problem for Pat and some other transsexuals as well.

Most people are under the impression that taking female hormones will have sudden and dramatic effects on the male body. This is not the case. The effects occur over a long period of time, and they are subtle in nature. Neither do they affect everyone to the same extent or in the same way. We all have different body chemistries, so we all react somewhat differently to various drugs introduced into our bodies.

Before we proceed further, there is one widely held myth I should like to put to rest. For years people have made jokes to the effect that if a man is kicked hard enough in the testicles, or for some reason he becomes castrated, or he takes female hormones, he will wind up with a soprano voice. The administration of estrogenic hormones or the removal of the male testes has absolutely no effect on the male voice, if the hormones are given or the testes removed beyond puberty. If estrogenic hormones are given (which effectively cause chemical castration) or the testes are removed from a pre-pubescent male, the vocal cords will not undergo normal male muscular development and the voice will retain a level of pitch usually associated with women. The vocal cords are muscle tissue and for the purpose of this discussion can be compared to the strings on a piano. Try to remember looking at the inside of a piano, and you will recall that the short, thin strings produce the high notes, and the long, thick strings produce the low notes. At the time of puberty, the hormone testosterone is produced by the male testes. It affects the vocal cords, stimulating them to elongate and become thicker. This is what provides the male with the typically deep voice. Women produce a small amount of testosterone from their adrenal glands, but it is usually not enough to cause changes in the vocal cord muscles. The basic effect this hormone has on women is to generate adequate sex drive.

When air passes between the vocal cords, they vibrate and produce sound in much the same manner that a piano string does when struck with the hammer. The longer and thicker the vocal cords are, the lower the rate of vibration and pitch. The shorter and thinner the vocal cords are, the higher the pitch. Once puberty has occurred and the vocal cords have grown longer and thicker, they remain this way for life: it is an irreversible process. This is the primary reason men frequently have great difficulty emulating the female voice when they present themselves as women. On the other hand, if a female to male transsexual takes the male hormone testosterone, her vocal cords will tend to thicken and grow longer; and physiologically she will acquire a voice more like a man's. The reverse process is not possible with men and, as a consequence, male-to-female transsexuals often have voice problems to overcome.

The reason male-to-female transsexuals' voices seem to change when they begin to pursue gender congruity has nothing to do with hormones. The changes are the result of personal efforts on their part. Many study with Speech and Language Pathologists and spend hours practicing with tape recorders.

Voice pitch is only one aspect of speech. Men and women tend to have different speech patterns as well as pitch differentials. Generally speaking, women use more correct English, they tend to speak more softly, they usually expell more air with their speech, and their speech often sounds more breathy as a result. Women often use more range in their voices and have higher highs and lower lows. Women also raise and lower their pitch at different places in sentences than men do. Men usually speak in more of a monotone, while women use more musical speech patterns. Women also use certain words and expressions men seldom use. Men tend to use more hostile-state verbs than do women. On the other hand, women are inclined to qualify their statements more so than men. There are many other differences in speech between men and women which have little to do with pitch, and the reader can easily see that many of these differences can be learned and applied to practical speech. With a slight raise in pitch, and a knowledge of and practice in using more typically female speech patterns, most male voices can be adapted to more acceptable female voices.

In general, some effects which may occur in males taking female hormones will happen over many, many months and years of treatment. Some breast development may take place. In some persons there is considerable development, and the results can be dramatic. In others, very little development takes place. It is thought this is controlled by individual genetic makeup, and the results are not at all predictable.

Over a long period of time, the male libido will diminish, as will sexual potency. Less ejaculatory fluid will be produced, because the estrogen tends to atrophy the prostate gland, the seminal vesicles, and the testes which produce semen. If estrogen is taken long enough, the prostate, seminal vesicles, and testes will usually stop producing semen altogether, and potency will completely disappear. Over a long period of time, the testes and the cord-like structures to the rear of the testes called the epididymis will tend to atrophy as well. The testes produce most of the hormone testosterone as well as sperm; as they atrophy, less testosterone will be produced. With a reduction of testosterone and a constant supply of female hormones in the system, other areas of the body may slowly be affected. Frequently muscle mass is reduced, and the general musculature takes on a softer, smoother appearance. Sometimes general fat distribution takes on a more feminine pattern but not always. As time goes on, body hair may become a little finer and reduced in density. Estrogen usually causes skin pores to become smaller, and a smoother complexion results. In general, the body takes on a softer tone.

There are many things which do not happen as a result of taking female hormones. The width of the pelvis is genetically determined and influenced by hormones at puberty as well.

By the time one is an adult, the pelvis is a rigid structure, and this will not change.

Scalp hair lost to male-pattern baldness will not regenerate. Estrogen will prevent the onset or halt the progress of male pattern baldness, however. If estrogen is taken before the cells die, regrowth of those hairs is possible; but once the hair cells are dead, hormones will not bring them back to life. Dead is dead. Many stories are told regarding hair regrowth after taking estrogen, but from a medical point of view, this seems most unlikely. Transsexuals who build up such expectations are very likely to be disappointed.

Female hormones will not alter the voice of a male with respect to pitch or speech patterns.

Female hormones will not change a person's way of walking or posture.

In short, the effects of female hormones are subtle and not very dramatic. Taken over a long period of time, they will cause some significant physiological changes, but taken by adults past puberty, they have little power to cause any significant structural, anatomical changes.

Many male-to-female transsexuals who begin hormone therapy report that the hormones have a calming effect on them, and they seem to reduce tension and anxiety. Whether this is due to bio-chemical changes, or to the placebo effect, is not clear. It may well be a combination of these two factors.

Androgenic, male hormones have a much more dramatic effect on genetic females than do estrogenic hormones on genetic males. Some of these changes take place in a few, short months. Beard and body hair growth patterns are stimulated, and female-to-male transsexuals develop these patterns rather quickly. When I interviewed Ed, he had not started taking male hormones. At that time he had a rather high-pitched, very typical female voice. About eight months after the interview I talked to him on the phone, I had no idea with whom I was talking. He had a very resonant, deep baritone voice, and I found it hard to believe this was the same person I had interviewed.

Testosterone will stop menstruation, usually by the next cycle after it is first administered. Most female-to-male transsexuals who had taken hormones told me the testosterone had tremendously stimulated their clitorises. Not only did they grow in length, but these transsexuals also reported a marked increase in their sexual drives. The latter statement would certainly appear to have a sound medical foundation. Testosterone is secreted by the adrenal glands in women in very small amounts, and it is what provides women with their libidos. Most of the individuals interviewed who were taking hormones also told me they were much stronger physically than they were before taking the hormones.

Other less dramatic and more subtle changes seem to take place when female to male transsexuals take male hormones. Many indicated they had an increase in acne; two told me they now had different body odors; many reported a loss of subcutaneous fat tissue; some indicated that their skin had become rougher; a few also told me they had a higher energy level, and two were developing male pattern baldness. Some reported that they had become much less emotional than they used to be and, similarly to male-to-female transsexuals, many said the hormones had a tranquilizing effect on them.

Androgenic and estrogenic hormones can have very powerful effects on the human body, and the decision to take them should be weighed carefully. Should a man or woman who believes he or she is a transsexual take hormones, and later discover he or she is not in fact a transsexual, or does not want to pursue gender congruity, some effects may be irreversible. If a woman who takes testosterone has her voice deepen and grows a beard, her beard would not disappear, and the voice would not change upward again if she stopped taking hormones. The only way she could resolve those problems would be the same way male-to-female transsexuals cope with them. She would have to learn to use her voice differently, and undergo expensive, painful electrolysis to remove the hair. The hormones might also render her infertile. If a man takes estrogen and enough atrophy of the testes and prostate gland occurs, even though he stops taking the hormone he may be sterile, impotent, or both.

Earlier in this chapter I indicated that sex hormones can sometimes have serious side effects. That is why it is important for physicians to keep close track of persons who are taking these hormones and monitor such bodily functions as blood pressure, liver function, and levels of fatty acids in the blood. In the case of the liver, alcohol can create additional stress, and a heavy drinker who takes hormones will probably be more at risk of causing liver damage. All of us are different of course, so each individual reacts a little differently. That is why close medical supervision of those taking hormones is very important.

After a pre-operative transsexual has been on hormone therapy, cross–living for at least one year, and continues to want to pursue gender congruity, that person then must be evaluated before genital surgery is performed. If the patient is recommended for surgery, the next phase of gender congruity is undertaken. This is, by far, the most serious step transsexuals take. Genital surgery is irreversible in the case of male to–female transsexuals, although that is not necessarily the case with female-to-male transsexuals. Female-to-male transsexuals must undergo a series of operations, and genital surgery for them has not been perfected to the degree that it has for male-to-female transsexuals. I will discuss first the male-to female surgery, and then describe the much more complex procedures female–to–male transsexuals have to undergo.

Most people are under the impression that when male to female genital surgery is performed, the penis and the testicles are removed. That is not entirely accurate. The ultimate goal of the surgery is to create a functional, cosmetically normal appearing vagina. This surgery is performed in a number of different ways. The least common method used is the transplantation of an ilial loop from the intestine to form the walls of the vagina. The testes and epididymis tissue are removed, an opening is made to the rear of this area, and the loop is inserted to form the lining of the vagina. This type of surgery has the advantage of providing a lining which is natural mucous membrane, and it will self-lubricate, as does a normal vagina. The operation requires abdominal surgery as well as genital surgery, however, so a great deal more patient risk is involved.

A far more common method of surgery involves the same procedure I have just described, except that the vagina is lined with skin transplanted from the thighs. It does not, of course, involve abdominal surgery. The one advantage this surgery offers is that enough skin can be transplanted to form a very large vagina. There are two disadvantages, I have been told, to this type of surgery. Firstly, the skin used to form the vagina is not erectile tissue; therefore, it will not be as responsive to sexual stimulation as erectile skin. Secondly, quite visible scars are left at the site from which the transplanted tissue was removed.

Probably the most common surgery at this time is called penile inversion. Again, the testes and epididymis tissue are removed. Instead of transplanting tissue from another area of the body, however, the skin of the penis is used to form the lining of the vagina. The only drawback to this type of surgery is that if the penis is not very large to begin with, there may not be enough penile skin to form a vagina which is functionally deep. The skin transplant method has to be used in that case. In all three of these surgical procedures, scrotal tissue is used to form the vulva.

Male-to-female genital surgery has existed in this country since June of 1965. In the beginning, the surgery was, of course, totally experimental in that techniques had to be developed. It has come a long way in the intervening years, and today the results are a tribute to modern plastic surgery. Male to-female genital surgery has reached a point where an artificially constructed vagina is very difficult to detect from a genetic one. A number of former transsexuals have told me they have been examined by physicians without those physicians suspecting that they ever had genital surgery. The cosmetic effect can be superb, and many former transsexuals have convinced doctors that they are women who have had hysterectomies.

Functionally, a large majority of former male-to-female transsexuals I talked to seemed quite satisfied. Most told me that they enjoyed sexual relations and were able to achieve climax. The greater number said they had to use some extra lubrication during sexual intercourse, but this did not seem to cause any real problems for them. Interestingly enough, three of the women who had the penile inversion type of surgery told me that they self-lubricate and need no additional lubrication during sexual intercourse. Genetic females have two small glands called the Bartholin's glands on either side of the vaginal orifice. They secrete a substance which provides lubrication for the penis as it enters the vagina. In addition, the cervix and the lining of the vagina secrete mucus which aids in lubrication of the vagina. When a woman becomes sexually aroused, the glandular and mucus secretions accelerate, and provide a very receptive atmosphere for the penis to penetrate. I asked an endocrinologist why these three former transsexuals might self-lubricate, and he told me that there is no scientific answer, but he has had a number of patients where this is the case. The human body is fascinating in its adaptability, and tissues somehow have the ability to take over functions that they were not originally intended to perform in some instance.

Two former male-to-female transsexuals I talked to had vaginas which had completely closed and were not capable of being penetrated. After the male to female genital surgery is performed, all patients must perform some sort of dilation of the vagina to keep it open and large enough during the healing period. This is done by inserting some sort of vaginal stent into the vagina. Some surgeons request that the stent be left in place and only removed when the person goes to the bathroom. Other surgeons request that the stent (such as a dildo) be inserted into the vagina periodically throughout the day. This is usually done about five times a day for periods of twenty minutes duration. A soft, inflatable stent is used for the first several weeks following surgery, and then the former patient must switch to a more firm, dildo-like device. This dilation must be done with frequency and usually for about six months. Dilation is the most critical post-operative procedure which must be followed, and it must be done religiously. Many a former transsexual patient has neglected this aspect of her care and found herself with a non-functional vagina. Should the vagina close completely, dangerous health hazards could result. Dilation performed so frequently is not an easy procedure to follow, and it takes a great deal of determination to keep it up.

Pain after male-to-female genital surgery varies from one person to another. Generally speaking, however, there is a great deal of pain for a time, and then the pain will subside sonewhat, leaving in its place a good deal of painful discomfort. As tissues slowly heal, much of the painful discomfort fades, but inserting a stent five times a day causes a lot of irritation to tender tissue, and there is a fair amount of discomfort for a number of months following surgery. The discomfort seems to diminish as the months go by and frequent dilating becomes less necessary. By the time six months pass and dilating no longer has to be a dominant feature in the lives of former transsexuals, most discomfort seems to disappear. Some individuals experience a certain amount of discomfort long after, and some do not.

Everyone is interested in orgasm these days. We all talk about it, analyze it, and try to have it. It seems that no respectable women's magazine goes to press these days without including an article on orgasm. Unless a woman is monitored by machines under laboratory conditions, statistics do not mean very much, as orgasm is a personal and highly subjective experience. Answers to questions I put to former male-to female transsexuals seem to indicate that these women achieve orgasm at least with the same frequency as genetic females. Be that as it may, it is very likely, putting aside any possible physical causes, that former male-to-female transsexuals will probably be orgasmic if they are sexually oriented to begin with.

Many surgeons who perform genital surgery also offer other types of cosmetic surgery, sometimes in conjunction with the genital surgery. Some male-to-female transsexuals have ancillary, cosmetic surgery performed prior to or after they have genital surgery, but some have everything done at one time. Of course many transsexuals only have genital surgery, and feel no need to have additional surgery. Frequently estrogen does not provide male-to-female transsexuals with a bust line they consider satisfactory. Many, therefore, have breast augmentation surgery. This is a procedure where a self-contained sack of silicone or saline solution is placed between the breast tissue and the pectoral muscles. This is a common cosmetic operation which many genetic females have performed as well. One of the drawbacks to this surgery is that there is sometimes a considerable loss of nerve sensation in the breasts, particularly in the area of the nipples. Another possible disadvantage to this type of surgery is that sometimes scar tissue forms around the sacks, and this causes the breasts to become rather hard and rigid. Self-image seems to be an overriding factor to many women, however, and they are willing to sacrifice physical sensation or run the risk of having scar tissue form for the sake of appearance.

Quite a few male-to-female transsexuals have some cosmetic facial surgery performed to enhance their looks. The most common of these surgeries is quite often asked for by genetic women as well. It is called rhinoplasty. It is usually desired to reduce the size of the nose or to alter a somewhat asymetrical one. It is a relatively simple procedure, with minor discomfort involved. The same can be said for reducing the size of the Adam's apple. Many genetic males have rather prominent Adam's apples, and this is considered a dead giveaway by some transsexuals. The procedure only takes a few moments and is usually covered with a bandaid for a few days.

Some male−to−female transsexuals become so fanatic about their appearances that they are willing to submit to almost any procedure which will enhance their feminine appearances. I know of former transsexuals who have gone to the extreme of having all the bones in their fingers broken and reset to provide a more dainty appearance. Some search out surgeons to have surgery on the hip and buttocks region to provide them with more feminine forms, and some have the bones beneath their eyebrows shaved to reduce protrusions. Most people want to have a pleasant self-image of themselves, but the average male-to-female transsexual cannot afford to have all these procedures done, even if they are desired. Genital surgery, sometimes combined with breast augmentation, rhinoplasty, or both, usually will give male to female transsexuals the desired effects.

Female-to-male transsexuals are faced with entirely different surgical problems. Genitally, there is nothing to be removed and little to be reshaped. Female-to-male transsexuals have to undergo a number of serious surgical procedures, and genital surgery is usually the last step. The most obvious, outward sign of gender identity with females are their breasts. Having breasts and what to do about it is usually the first priority of female-to-male transsexuals. For most women, their breasts confirm their femininity, and the loss of one or both of them to a disease such as cancer is a traumatic event. The majority of women, under those circumstances, need some peer counseling and sometimes professional assistance as well. Most women come to terms with their losses and regain positive images of themselves as women, but some are never able to accommodate to such circumstances. They feel they are less than full women, and never recapture inner peace in terms of their gender identity. Perhaps it is a little easier to understand the feelings transsexuals have if we view them from the point of view of women who loose one or both breasts. We only have to "flip the picture over," and we can begin to see the plight of transsexuals. When someone identifies themself internally as male, and yet has the most prominent badge of femininity (breasts), but lacks the most obvious sign of masculinity (a penis), perhaps the internal conflict which goes on becomes understandable. When someone else identifies themself internally as female, yet has the most obvious sign of masculinity, but lacks the most prominent feature of femininity, we can understand the driving force behind transsexuals submitting themselves to grueling and painful hours of electrolysis, the risks of hormone therapy, and the knife of a surgeon. I can think of no better way to explain the feelings involved than to ask the reader to imagine the lack of or the loss of sexual organs or characteristics which maintain your gender identity internally, and in the eyes of the world; and it must be kept in mind that these feelings are not sudden, whimsical fantasies transsexuals decide to act out. In most cases, the feelings have been present since very early childhood.

Breast reduction surgery is very expensive, and female-to male transsexuals often go to great lengths to hide their breasts until they can afford to have them removed. Many of the persons I interviewed were binding their breasts and wearing very loose tops (almost all the female to male transsexuals I interviewed who had not had bilateral mastectomies at the time of the interview have since had that surgery). Breast binding is very uncomfortable, as the reader can imagine; but most female-to-male transsexuals would rather do this than have their breasts be obvious, particularly in the cross living stage. So the first order of business for female-to-male transsexuals is to have a bilateral mastectomy. This surgery usually requires only one to three nights in the hospital, but there is quite a bit of pain and discomfort afterward. These patients have to be very careful about arm movement so that stitches will not be torn. There is also a fair amount of risk of post-surgical infection developing from this type of surgery, and that too must be guarded against. The principal problem with this procedure, as expressed to me by those who have had it, is that most surgeons are not experienced in creating a cosmetically attractive, masculine appearing chest. Many surgeons experienced in breast reduction are used to operating on women who want to maintain as feminine an appearance as possible after the surgery; they often seek breast implants after the surgery when the mastectomy has not been to radical, and there is enough muscle and skin tissue left to allow for effective implants. When implants are not possible, many women still will use some sort of breast prothesis to provide a pleasing, cosmetic appearance to enhance their self-image, and for clothing to fit properly. Of course some women have breast reduction because they have very large or pendulous breasts which become physically uncomfortable. In either case, these women want to retain their feminine appearances. As a consequence, few surgeons have tackled the problem of mastectomy from the point of view of leaving scars in unobtrusive places and creating more masculine appearing chests. A number of persons I talked to told me they would never take their shirts off in public, because their chests were badly scarred or still had feminine appearances to them. On the other hand, some surgeries are not at all noticeable. Bob, a female-to-male transsexual, had his shirt off the day I interviewed him. It was very hot that day, and he was just being comfortable. Bob had so much hair all over his body that it would have been difficult to see any scars, even if any were prominent. Bob looked like any normal male I have seen without a shirt and was much more hirsute than the average man.

Most female-to-male transsexuals I talked to eventually planned to have hysterectomies so that their uteruses and ovaries could be removed. This, of course, is major abdominal surgery, in most cases, but it is desireable to female-to-male transsexuals, because the ovaries are the principal manufacturer of estrogen. One man had decided not to have this procedure, because he felt the contractions of his uterus at the time of climax enhanced that experience; he did not want to risk losing any of the pleasurable effects of orgasm.

When these two major surgeries are out of the way, the female-to-male transsexual is still faced with the problem of having a vagina and no penis. At the present time, there is no known way a vagina can be converted to a penis. The female clitoris is considered to be homologous with the penis of the male. By that, physicians mean it is corresponding in structure, position, origin, etc. Many of the female-to-male transsexuals I interviewed indicated that they intended only to have the hoods of their clitorises removed, let the hormones stimulate their growth, and simply consider them as penises but not functional for intercourse. A few of them told me their clitorises had grown to lengths equal to their thumbs, anywhere from one and three quarters inches to two and one half inches. The reason they had made these decisions was that they did not consider the present genital surgery satisfactory and were willing to wait until some of the existing shortcomings of the surgery were overcome.

The surgical procedure to form a penis is called a phaloplasty, and it is accomplished by one of several methods of skin grafting. Skin, usually from the lower portion of the abdomen, is formed into the shape of a flap, and it is then transplanted to the pubic area. This surgical procedure has many drawbacks, as one can imagine. Firstly, the transplanted tissue has few nerve endings, so the penis has almost no sensation. Secondly, ejaculation is not possible. Thirdly, a prosthetic device must be inserted into the penis to make it rigid for sexual intercourse. Fourthly, urinary tract infections are common when attempts are made to extend the urethra by means of prosthetic devices through the penis to allow for urination in a standing position.

94

Quite a bit of research is being conducted at the present time to develop surgical techniques which do not have the drawbacks I have mentioned. It is my understanding that one clinic in the United States has developed and is using micro-surgery to perform the phaloplasty. From the reports I have received, it is considered extremely effective and success-fully overcomes many of the limitations of conventional sur-gery. I have also been told it is extremely expensive so unless costs come down or medical insurance covers this surgery, most female-to-male transsexuals will not be able to afford this latest development.

Sometimes before, but usually after, a phaloplasty is com-pleted, surgeons can utilize the vulva to form a scrotal sack and implant spherical, silicone devices in the sack to provide a natural appearing set of testicles. I have talked to a number of men who have had phaloplasties. All these men told me that they were very satisfied with the surgery and that the phaloplasties were effective during sexual intercourse. Al-though former female-to-male transsexuals who have had phaloplasties cannot ejaculate, they are perfectly capable of orgasms from clitoral stimulation. Other female-to-male transsexuals I interviewed told me, in their opinions, the sur-gery left much to be desired cosmetically and functionally. It certainly seems clear that genital surgery for female-to-male transsexuals is far behind in development compared to the genital surgery available for male-to-female transsexuals. This may, in part, be due to the fact that male-to-female transsex-uals received most of the attention in the early days of gen-der congruity surgery, but gender congruity surgery for fe-male-to-male transsexuals presents many more difficult sur-gical problems.

If I were to cite costs for gender congruity, the figures I might present would be out of date by the time this book be-comes available to the reader. The cost of medical care in the United States has been steadily rising and continues to rise even in periods of low inflation. Suffice it to say the costs for gender congruity, particularly gender congruity surgery, are astronomical and well beyond the reach of most people. Almost no help is available from Medicaid, and very few health insurance companies will cover surgical costs. Some insurance companies specifically exclude gender congruity surgery from their policies. Others classify it as elective and therefore not eligible for benefit payment; other companies classify the surgery as experimental and therefore ineligible for benefit payment.

There is a moral climate in this country which allows the type of regulations I have been discussing to exist. Many physicians themselves have a moralistic opposition to gender congruity. Certainly no one should prevent them from holding those views, and they should not be obliged to provide treatment which is abrasive to their personal sense of morality. On the other hand, I have serious qualms when they wish to impose their morality on others who do not view gender congruity as a moral issue. I also sense blatant hypocrisy when people in or out of the medical profession present moral objections to gender congruity, whether it is weakly put forth as rules and regulations or it is open confrontation with the process. Somehow it seems ludicrous and ironic that some persons in our society would frown on a person who had breasts, felt they stood in the way of his masculine identity, and had those breasts removed, but those same judgmental persons most certainly would approve of a genetic male having breast reduction surgery if he suffered from gynocomastia (enlarged breasts on a male). They also would not object to someone having a hypospadiac condition corrected (hypospadia is a birth defect where the urethra protrudes from the bottom of the penis, usually near the pubis). I cannot for the life of me understand why certain persons in society should feel they have the right to be judge and jury concerning other people's internal gender identity. That is what they become, in effect, when they disapprove of transsexuals having surgery. They say: "We don't care how you feel inside, we are not going to let modern science help you, because we don't think it is right." What they really mean is: the transsexual phenomenon makes them very uncomfortable, because they do not understand it; they are willing to see lives wasted, because they do not quite know how to cope with the phenomenon in their own minds.

Many opponents of gender congruity bring up the subject of religion and make statements such as: "God made you the way you are and you have no right to change that." But where are their protests when hopelessly disabled persons are given artificial limbs, joints, or heart valves? According to the logic of those religious protesters, people should not be allowed to take advantage of many of the advances in modern medicine, because "God made these people the way they are." Where are their protests when diabetics are injected with insulin derived from animals? Where are their protests when tiny babies, days, weeks, and only months old, in some cases, are operated on to have birth or genetic defects corrected? Where are their cries, "God made you that way" when Siamese twins are separated by surgery so that they can live whole, normal lives? Certainly if God made transsexuals, that same God must have made Siamese twins. The implication here, of course, is that transsexuals choose to be the way they are, while others with physical or developmental birth or genetic defects and persons who develop medical conditions do not make choices. That is patent nonsense. No one chooses to be a transsexual any more than anyone chooses to be a diabetic. It is beyond comprehension to think that someone would choose to have feelings which would take him or her down a path of social, financial, and emotional trauma. My research, and the research of many others, clearly show that transsexuals do not choose to be transsexuals. Lin Fraser, a therapist in San Francisco, California, who specializes in working with transgendered persons, told me that in her entire career she had never met a true transsexual who chose to be one. The *only choice* involved for transsexuals is what to do about their conditions. The individuals who argue against surgical intervention for transsexuals on religious or moral grounds use spurious arguments and are hypocritical in the worst sense. They claim to follow the precepts of Jesus who preached the love of God and fellow man, and yet they are perfectly willing to turn their backs on their fellow man and condemn some to an internal hell based on their personal interpretations of what is right or wrong. They seek to create a moral monopoly and dictate to others how they should think, feel, and behave. These individuals have little sense of a compassionate and caring God. They are nothing more than moral fascists, and their pseudo-moral harangues should be considered with that in mind. It would behoove those moral adjudicators to keep their own spiritual yards free of weeds instead of constantly spading in other people's gardens.

# Chapter 9
# FABRIC OF MIND,
# THE WARP AND WOOF

Herrica was thirty years old when I interviewed her. In her mid-twenties she discovered a shocking reality. "I read an article in a pornographic magazine about transsexualism when I was about twenty-six. I had never heard of transsexualism, or Christine Jorgensen before. I went into a state of disattachment with my surroundings, and said to myself, 'Hey! This is what I am!' It literally devastated me for two years. I thought I knew myself so well, this discovery completely destroyed my self-image. I didn't want the problems I could envision, and to be considered weird and perverse. I became very depressed, and ended up quitting my job."

It seems hard to believe, in this day and age, someone could reach the age of twenty-six, yet have no inkling he or she might be a transsexual, particularly someone as bright and as well-educated as Herrica is. When I asked her about this and pointed out that she must have had some feelings in the past which might have made her suspicious, she told me that she did have some feelings and desires at an early age that she might want to be a female; but she just dismissed them, put them in her "Herrica is different" bin and really did not give them further thought.

Although over eighty–five percent of the transsexuals I interviewed had some form of gender discomfort before they ever started school, many of them did not recognize that discomfort as transsexualism until much later in life. Bob told me, "Even though I read about Christine Jorgenson, I didn't really relate it to myself. When I finally did, it felt like my head was taken out of a vise." Edward: "When I did finally find out about transsexualism, it was like finding a missing link, or the musical chord I had been searching for. I was ecstatic to find out I could define myself and do something about my condition. I was walking on air." Kitty: "I knew about transsexualism since I was thirteen or fourteen. I always thought it was shameful. I tried for many years to find a way around it and to fight my feelings. No matter what I did, though (including trying to get in the service), my feelings just didn't change." Karen: "I knew about transsexualism as I was growing up, but wasn't sure it related to me. It took me a couple of years of psychotherapy to discover I was, in fact, a transsexual. I really didn't discover it until I was in my early thirties."

If we could be like the proverbial fly on the wall in the office of a therapist who specializes in treating persons with gender problems, the remarks of Bob, Edward, Kitty, and Karen would become very familiar indeed. Having feelings and recognizing the significance of those feelings do not necessarily go hand in hand. Helping persons sort out their feelings, recognize what those feelings may mean, learning to feel okay about having those feelings without a tremendous burden of guilt, and figuring out ways to cope with their lives within the limitations of their feelings is probably an ideal formula for beneficial therapy. Many transsexuals seek out therapy without having the slightest idea they are transsexuals. They just recognize that all is not well in their lives and are searching for answers.

Of course not all transsexuals are as naive about their situations as Karen was. Some recognize that they are transsexuals but do now know how to cope with their situations. Frequently they will seek out therapists when they no longer can take the internal pressures of being transsexuals and are enduring emotional pain and stress beyond their limits of toleration. Many of these transsexuals realize that they have to do something about their situations, but they are afraid and tentative. They may never have tried cross-living, and often they do not believe they could ever pass in opposite gender roles. These individuals often know they are flirting with the possibility of altering their entire lives and, perhaps, losing the friendship and love of the ones who mean the most to them. Some also face the possibility of losing their sources of income and perhaps undergoing a great deal of public and private humiliation. They know that society, in general, does not take the plight of transsexuals seriously, and they have every reason to be afraid. Only about one person in four or five who starts the cross-living experiment carries forward to the point where they have genital surgery and live the rest of their lives in opposite gender roles. Those certainly are not very good odds, and transsexuals must have a lot of things going for them in order to overcome such poor odds. The odds I mentioned, of course, do not take into account whether they will be able to live happy and successful lives after the surgery and adjust to new gender roles. One very controversial report (The Meyer Report) was issued on a follow-up of former transsexuals (this report is discussed in some detail in Chapter 10). The report was very negative in its findings and concluded that little benefit was gained from gender congruity surgery over conventional psychotherapy. That report, however, was flawed in a number of ways and has been thoroughly refuted by other, very credible social scientists. According to Dr. Paul Walker, not nearly enough material has been accumulated through follow-up studies of former transsexuals in order to draw any valid, statistical conclusions. A number of studies are underway at the present time, and in a few years there should be some reliable stastical data available. Dr. Walker has rightfully pointed out that persons who are successful in completing gender congruity are difficult to follow-up on, because they just tend to blend into society. They do not want to send progress reports to physicians or other researchers every six months, and that is certainly understandable in light of their goals of living their lives in gender roles other than ones they were assigned at birth. Unlike homosexuals who make the decision to "come out of the closet" and open up their lives publicly, transsexuals usually want to close the doors of the past and get on about their lives in their new gender roles. They know they would stand little chance of leading any kind of normal lives if they were to reveal their situations to any but their most intimate, trusted friends and loved ones.

Probably the most important reason for homosexuals to come out of the closet is to gain self-respect and try to purge some of the guilt and anxiety they have experienced for having feelings not acceptable to a large segment of society. Many persons would prefer that homosexuals just stay in the closet and not bother society. Even today, there are others who would condemn homosexuals in the name of God, while some would gladly invade the privacy of homosexuals and throw them in jail because they are acting upon their feelings. Very recently I have heard some individuals say that Acquired Immune Deficiency Syndrome (better known as AIDS) is God's way of punishing homosexuals for their sexual practices. If this is true, then I suppose we have to assume that various sexually transmitted diseases are God's punishment of heterosexuals for their sexual practices. One has to wonder what God is punishing people for who develop Muscular Dystrophy or, until vaccine was developed, Polio. This kind of logic boggles the mind and is pure rubbish. I do not think this is the type of God most people in our society embrace. It has only been in the last ten to twenty years that many states have eliminated laws from their statutes prohibiting consenting adults from having sexual relations in the privacy of their own homes if those relations were not between males and females. These attitudes notwithstanding, the process of coming out of the closet for homosexuals is a healthy, psychological experience for those involved and for society as a whole. A healthy society is based upon individual freedoms, where exercising those freedoms does not interfere with the rights and freedoms of others. The responsibility of freedom carries with it the necessity of being tolerant of others and their preferences, whether we personally approve or not. If we abandon those responsibilities, we open the door to repression and totalitarianism.

When we examine the plight of transsexuals, the act of coming out of the closet becomes a much more complex issue. Most social scientists are in agreement that about ten percent of the population, worldwide at any given time, is homosexual. Although some social scientists feel this number is too high, all agree that the figure is probably somewhere between five and ten percent. Ten percent, if that figure is reasonably close, is one out of every ten persons, and that is a very significant portion of society. In recent years, homosexuals have come to realize that there is power in numbers, and they have effectively joined forces in many areas to achieve significant political power and to create major changes in laws and societal attitudes. It must also be kept in mind that homosexuals are of one mind when it comes to their sexual preferences. They are all attracted to members of their own gender. Quite a different situation exists for transsexuals. Although there are no very reliable figures regarding the number of transsexuals in our society, we do know that they comprise only a very small fraction of less than one percent of the population. Even though transsexualism is sensationalized and often creates headlines, the facts that it involves such fundamental concepts and is so rare are precisely the reasons it is often in the news. Transsexuals are few and far between; consequently, they simply do not have sufficient numbers to form any sort of political power base. Even more important than numbers, however, is the reality that transsexuals do not have the one, cohesive bond all homosexuals have. Although some transsexuals are homosexual, and some are bisexual, the vast majority of them are heterosexual. The glue which helps to bind the homosexual community does not exist for transsexuals. Homosexuals are fighting for the right to lead alternative life-styles based on sexual preference; they ask that they be given the same rights, freedoms, and privileges which others enjoy, even though they choose life-styles based on sexual preference. In most cases, transsexuals do not want to be a part of any group in relation to sexual preference or any other one particular cause, except what their individual societal interests may dictate. They want to be part of the community of man and be able to live their lives as men and women. In most cases, they do not want to be identified as a minority group. Coming out of the closet may have some psychological benefits for some transsexuals in terms of coping with guilt, but it offers little in the way of community support the way it can for homosexuals. Homosexuals often take pride in having the sexual preferences they do, much in the same manner that black Americans promoted the concept of "black is beautiful" when the civil rights movement flowered in the ninteen sixties. Transsexuals, on the other hand, simply want to go on about their business and live their lives as men and women. Most transsexuals or former transsexuals very much want to live within the bounds of society, rather than living what some might call alternative life-styles. Of course it would be ideal if transsexuals were able to acknowledge their dilemmas publicly, go through the process of gender congruity, and easily be accepted by an open, understanding society. Unfortunately these conditions do not exist at present, and most transsexuals prefer to guard their secrets rather than expose themselves to public ridicule.

Some transsexuals and former transsexuals elect to be open about their situations and have the attitude that persons who cannot accept their situations are not worth knowing; they will only associate with those who will accept them for what they are. Some of these transsexuals and former transsexuals soon find that complete forthrightness with everyone they come in contact with creates problems for them, and they learn to be judicious in deciding who they take into their confidence. Others continue to fight the world and often lead very unhappy lives. The sad fact is few people know anything at all about transsexualism, and many will withdraw if persons do identify themselves as transsexuals. I have pointed out several times that the whole subject has been greatly distorted and sensationalized by the media. The public has every reason to be hesitant and skeptical about transsexualism in view of the way it has been presented. The image is further enhanced, in all fairness, by some self-proclaimed transsexuals and diagnosed transsexuals who exhibit bizarre or anti-social behavior. Is it any wonder that the public is confused when an article is headlined, "TRANSVESTITE DANCE HALL'S PERMIT BID DELAYED AGAIN", and the following paragraph appears in the story?

> . . . "He characterized McCannon as a 'good woman' who has 'loaned money for sex change operations' to many patrons of her bar" . . .*

Another story appeared in the San Francisco Chronicle on Monday, March 22, 1982. There was a picture of two persons dressed as women, and the caption under the picture was, "ALL DRESSED UP." Under the caption were a few lines explaining the picture and the caption.

> " 'Joan' (left) and 'Bobby' are two satisfied subscribers to a new enterprise in Seattle: The Transvestite Contact Service, whose operators claim it is the nation's first dating service for transvestites and transsexuals. 'Joan,' (sic) who said he has always felt like a woman, is preparing for a sex change operation; 'Bobby' is a cross-dressing (sic) hairdresser who recently moved west from New York."

Perhaps we cannot fault a reporter who writes stories such as these, but certainly the judgment of their editors can and should be questioned. Several excellent articles on the subject of transsexualism have appeared in newspapers and magazines in the last several years. A good example is a two part article which appeared in the San Francisco Chronicle on Monday, November 30, 1981, and Tuesday, December 1, 1981. This article covered many pages, and much of it was written by the Science Editor, David Perlman. The article was not only extensive but thorough. It clearly differentiated between transsexualism, transvestism, and homosexuality. The article was very well researched, and experts in the field such as Dr. Paul Walker were interviewed. Another example of a well-researched, clearly written article on the subject of transsexualism appeared in Family Circle Magazine in the May 15, 1979 issue. The article was written by Pamela Bujarski-Greene, a freelance writer.

*San Francisco Chronicle, Thursday, September 24, 1981      103

In view of articles such as the ones I have cited and appearances on national as well as local television programs of experts like Dr. Walker, it is difficult to excuse the media for continuing to publish and present information about transsexualism which is misleading, inaccurate, and often presented in a manner which perpetuates all sorts of half-truths and, in many instances, false information. As a consequence, it is not difficult to understand why the public continues to be confused about the subject and possesses little accurate information. We must not forget that transsexuals also are part of the reading and viewing public, and they all too often become confused and misled by some media coverage; certainly the negative sensationalism can create tremendous guilt by association when transsexuals are presented in bizarre ways along with misleading information.

There are transsexuals and others who feel they know exactly what they want, and only seek out therapists in order to fulfill the necessary requirements to be recommended for gender congruity surgery. They are often quite sophisticated in their knowledge of the Standards of Care and what therapists are looking for in order to make positive evaluations. Many of them will "play the game" with therapists to get the evaluation and will withold feelings or information from therapists which might set up doubts in the therapists' minds as to whether these persons are really prepared for surgery at that time. The Standards of Care I referred to in Chapter 5 do help to avoid this type of situation to a certain extent, but if patients are bright and informed, they frequently can get the results they desire. Experienced therapists often can pick up on these games, but some persons do slip through even the most capable and experienced therapists' probing. The sad part of all this is: the potential candidate for surgery, in the long run, is only putting himself or herself at tremendous risk when playing these games. Most therapists I have met who treat transsexuals are very dedicated and have the welfare of their patients uppermost in their minds. Many of the transsexuals I interviewed would disagree with this last observation. No doubt there are some therapists who are not responsible, but, by and large, it is my impression that most therapists do have the best interests of their patients at heart. Even the most capable of therapists cannot help, however, if the patients really do not want help and simply are interested in achieving certain goals they feel are correct despite what others might think. It is a little bit like cheating all the way through school. If students get away with it and get good grades, those grades may help them obtain good jobs in the world. What those students do not seem to realize is that good grades are not knowledge, and although they may obtain good jobs based on grades, the business world will expect them to perform in a manner commensurate with the abilities their grades are supposed to reflect. If they have obtained their grades by spurious methods instead of hard work, their job performances will soon reflect that fact, and they will quickly discover employers are interested in performance. In the counterpart of this analogy, transsexuals who play games and are not willing to examine themselves honestly in making such important decisions about their futures are very apt to encounter emotional disasters down the road.

As we enter the inner sanctum of the therapist's world, it already seems obvious that a high priority is to help patients sort out their problems and come to some realization of whether they have gender or sexual problems or both. Another top priority is to discover whether patients may have extraneous problems having little to do with gender confusion or gender discomfort. Many persons seek gender congruity for the wrong reasons. It is difficult to forget about Helen, the woman whose story I related in Chapter 2, when I mention that some who do not have true gender discomfort seek gender congruity. All these problems can be so interwoven that it sometimes takes years to sort them all out so that patients can make some reasonably clear assessments of what is the best course of action for themselves. And after all, it is the patients who must ultimately make the decisions. No one can tell anyone he or she is a transsexual. It is an inner sense of awareness, and it really cannot be diagnosed in the strictest sense, except by empirical evidence based mostly on observation. The best that therapists can do is to certify that the feelings transsexuals say they have seem to be verified after observing them in the cross-living stage. I think most therapists would agree that the best test of whether persons are transsexuals or not is to observe them in cross-living situations. If those persons can successfully adopt opposite gender roles from a social, occupational, and emotional standpoint, express happiness in the new roles, and a desire to continue in the roles, at that point they are probably good candidates for gender congruity surgery — provided other emotional or life problems do not stand in the way. Individuals, ultimately, must make the diagnoses and the decisions to have gender congruity surgery; all therapists can do is to    105 certify and confirm that some people are probably acting in their best interests in pursuing gender congruity surgery.

Nan, a woman about thirty-five years old, called me one evening when I was conducting interviews for this book. She told me that she was interested in being interviewed, but she very forthrightly said she was not sure whether she was in fact a female-to-male transsexual and was not sure I would be interested in her. I told her I certainly would like to talk to her, because Nan's story is a vivid illustration of how various factors can sometimes come together in people's lives which can cause them to consider pursuing gender congruity for the wrong reasons.

Nan was brought up in a fairly typical, middle-class American home, in so far as her age group is concerned. Her father is a professional man, and her mother did not work outside the home when Nan and her sister were growing up. That family situation, of course, would no longer be considered typical. Her parents are strict Catholics and very decent people, but there was little family warmth and affection between her parents or the children and their parents. Little discussion took place in the home regarding personal matters, and there just did not seem to be very much meaningful communication in the family. Nan's father was around the home quite a bit, but from the way Nan described his participation in the family, my impression was: although he was physically present, he was really an emotionally absent father. Of course this phenomenon is not unique to Nan's family, and many families live together in this fashion. In many cases, it would seem they are just going through the motions of being families, rather than living together, enjoying each other and the interaction which occurs in a close family.

Ideologically, Nan could probably best be described as a feminist. As she was growing up she was not very popular, but she developed an early interest in sports. When she was telling me about her feelings and how she resented the fact that boys' sports always took precedence over girls' sports, she became very emotional. I could not help but be very moved by the depth of her feelings and the internal suffering this discrimination caused her as a young girl. Her sense of inequality and belief that women are treated as second class citizens in our culture have carried over to her adult years; she identifies closely with the feminist movement.

Nan indicated to me that she felt she was probably a lesbian. Her sexual preference is only relevant in the sense that those who view themselves as homosexuals sometimes develop gender confusion. It turned out, in Nan's case, she was questioning her gender identity on the basis of her sexual preference and ideological beliefs. In short, Nan was deliberating the idea, not so much that she might be a transsexual but that maybe it would be desirable to become a transsexual. Nan's thinking was: if she were to become a man somehow through gender congruity, she could step up in the world and become a first-class citizen. She felt she would no longer be a target on the streets and would be treated with the respect she feels men get in this world and women do not.

I reminded Nan several times during our visit that one does not become a transsexual. I told her I had never met a transsexual who had chosen to be one and then became one. Some individuals, as I pointed out, discover they are transsexuals, and they may or may not elect to do something about it. Nan readily admitted that she identified as a woman; she just did not feel that being a woman in our culture was desirable because of societal attitudes. Nan had never cross-dressed; she never desired to be a boy or felt she was a boy when she was younger, and she candidly told me that the thought of any surgical procedures to change her body did not appeal to her at all. I told Nan I was not a therapist and not qualified to tell her whether she was or was not a transsexual. I did point out to her, however, that the background of feelings she related to me certainly did not appear to be at all similar to the feelings transsexuals had expressed to me in interviews. I also suggested that she should think long and hard if she were contemplating taking any hormones, as some of the effects could be permanent. I urged her to seek some professional counseling if she continued to entertain thoughts of "becoming a transsexual."

Nan, of course, could benefit from counseling even if she no longer feels gender congruity might solve her problems. She obviously has some real problems concerning her self-esteem as a woman. I certainly have no quarrel with her feminist beliefs and share many of them with her. But Nan's problems obviously cannot be resolved by changing her body or her role in society, no more so than Helen could eliminate her problems by becoming someone else. From my observations, transsexuals and former transsexuals really do not become different persons when they achieve gender congruity. The old shibboleth that leopards do not change their spots is, I think, applicable to former transsexuals. Dishonest persons do not become honest through gender congruity. Greedy persons do not suddenly become beneficent from gender congruity. Inconsiderate persons remain inconsiderate, even after gender congruity. Former transsexuals do change, certainly in appearance. Frequently, they also change in terms of their attitudes and behavior based on living in other gender roles. But my research did not indicate to me that the process of gender congruity has any effect on people's basic character values. Gender congruity, in many cases, does allow persons to flower and live life more fully than was previously possible for them. It often makes them more attractive, self-assured, and pleasant to be around, because they are more comfortable with themselves. I would have to characterize changes, other than obvious changes due to shifts in gender roles, as more of a growth process than anything else. Gender congruity requires a great deal of patience, perserverence, personal emotional strength, introspection, and stability; the development of those types of personal characteristics has a maturing effect on most individuals. Although the process is often very painful emotionally and physically, I have seen a number of persons I initially interviewed respond to the process by growing and developing into much more mature persons than when I interviewed them.

It is not uncommon for therapists to see members of transsexuals' families. It is usually quite helpful to therapists if they can consult family members to verify histories that transsexuals have given them and to gain perspectives other family members may have. Many times, they can provide therapists with information which can be of real benefit in therapy sessions. It also can give therapists a pretty clear picture of what attitudes transsexuals are facing from their loved ones, should they elect to pursue gender congruity.

Family counseling is often beneficial to the loved ones of transsexuals. Therapists can help them understand transsexuals' dilemmas and offer assurance that they may be heading down a path which could significantly improve the quality of their lives. Whenever possible, therapists will consult with loved ones and, in many cases, they can help loved ones learn to continue their love for transsexuals in opposite gender roles. All too often, people are under the impression that transsexuals pursue gender congruity for some perverse or whimsical sexual reason; they usually find it difficult to accept the fact that transsexualism is a long-standing problem for those involved or that transsexuals cannot solve their problems through psychotherapy. Sometimes, when loved ones are told the facts and learn that gender congruity may be the only way transsexuals can ever expect to live with any degree of comfort, they become more tolerant and supportive of those transsexuals. Some relationships, of course, cannot be salvaged, because their loved ones are adamantly opposed to the course of action these transsexuals are taking. Their feelings of anger at the transsexuals preclude any possibility that they might seek counseling in order to gain understanding. Frequently, however, therapists can provide real help to the loved ones of transsexuals when they are willing to try.

All of us are different and have different needs, temperaments, and capacities. The way transsexuals adjust to cross-role living is quite individualistic. Some easily adjust to cross living; some find it very difficult and painful; conversely, others are never able to adjust to living in roles in which they were not raised. Cross–dressing in public, let alone cross living, is a very frightening prospect for most transsexuals. Many are very unsure of themselves and convinced they will never be able to pass in opposite gender roles. In the beginning, all transsexuals are fearful to some extent that they somehow will be exposed and humiliated if they start cross dressing or cross-living. Therapists can play important roles in these situations by providing encouragement and support to those undertaking these experiments. Many of the transsexuals I interviewed also seemed to feel that peer counseling and encouragement was just as important under those circumstances, if not more so. No one, of course, should ever be encouraged to undertake cross-living unless he or she expresses a desire to do so, but if someone does, therapists and other transsexuals can be of real help. Most transsexuals are quite certain that other people are able to read them. Any words said by others which can possibly be construed by transsexuals that might question their gender will be interpreted that way by transsexuals. Even with proper documentation, transsexuals who are cross living live in fear of being arrested, having an accident, or encountering some situation beyond their control which will reveal their true gender. These are understandable fears, and they should be talked about with therapists. It is a very good idea for therapists to furnish letters to patients when they start to cross-live. The letters should state that the patients are under their care, being treated for gender dysphoria, and that part of the treatment requires them to live in opposite gender roles. It is also helpful for physicians who may be prescribing hormones to furnish patients with similar letters.

There are other, practical matters with which therapists can help transsexuals cope. Most therapists have knowledge of where transsexuals can find services they may need. Many male to female transsexuals need help with their voices, and therapists can refer them to Speech Pathologists who can assist them. Most male-to-female transsexuals need electrolysis for the removal of their beards; again, therapists can refer them to electrologists who will accept transsexuals. Male-to female and female-to-male transsexuals need to find physicians who are experienced in the medical treatment of them; and once again, therapists can make referrals. Most therapists are aware of support groups, rap groups, and individuals who may be of help to transsexuals. Therapists who are experienced in counseling transsexuals usually have knowledge of much practical information which can be of real benefit to their patients.

Sometimes, therapists will encounter persons who very likely are transsexuals, but for one of any number of reasons will not be able to successfully cross-live and pursue gender congruity through genital surgery. Physical size does not usually have to be a determining factor, but there are realities which have to be faced. If a male-to-female transsexual is six feet, six inches tall, weighs, perhaps, two hundred and fifty or sixty pounds, and has tattoos all over his body, that person is going to stand out and draw the eyes of the public. That would be true, of course, even if that person were a genetic female. But it is important for such a transsexual to understand that no matter what he does, he is going to be an object of continual interest to the general public. If a transexual who finds himself in this situation is realistic as to how he will be perceived in the female gender role and feels he can cope with those realities, that person may be a candidate for gender congruity surgery. Realistically, however, most people do not want to be the object of curiosity and possibly ridicule for the rest of their lives. Few would find life pleasant or be able to cope under those circumstances.

Often, male-to-female transsexuals may be quite large for women, but their attitudes and general demeanors will make it quite possible for them to live in female gender roles without attracting undue attention. Sometimes, male to female transsexuals may be quite small in size, but their attitudes, demeanors, and personal habits will preclude them from ever successfully living in female gender roles. I interviewed two persons like this, and no matter how hard they may try, I doubt that they ever will be able to overcome certain personality traits which would allow them to pass successfully in female roles.

Other transsexuals may have serious emotional problems which they never overcome, and those emotional problems can stand in the way of their pursuing gender congruity. Some transsexuals are so burdened with guilt or so committed to their family situations that they too may never be able to pursue gender congruity. In all of these situations, therapists face, perhaps, their greatest challenge: helping those who are not good candidates for gender congruity come to terms with their situations and work out solutions which will allow them to live happy and useful lives within the limitations of their feelings. Quite frankly, that is not a task I would want to undertake, and I have great admiration for therapists who can help people under such adverse circumstances.

Based on the problems I have heard from the transsexuals I interviewed and talked to, and the emotional trauma they frequently go through, my personal feeling is that transsexuals should be encouraged by therapists to explore any and all alternatives to gender congruity surgery. It certainly is a solution for a few, and it needs to be totally legitimized for them. Even then, those who do successfully pursue gender congruity through surgery endure a great deal of agonizing emotional pain and physical suffering as well. It leaves indelible scars which remain for life. Gender congruity should be a last resort, not a first option. If persons can find ways of living with some degree of comfort, each and every avenue should be thoroughly explored and tested. Gender congruity should be the court of last resort, and it should not be used as a small claims court. Ironically, a small claims court used in this manner can impose life sentences and exact high punitive damages; worst of all, there is no court of appeal, and no procedures for pardon or clemency. The sentences are final and forever.

# Chapter 10
# WHEN ALL IS SAID AND DONE

In Chapter 7 I stated that a glaring weakness in the transsexual process is the lack of information from readily available sources. Although this paucity of information can cause transsexuals much anxiety, loss of time, and difficulty in trying to come to grips with specific problems, its most devastating effect is on those who, for any number of reasons, should never pursue gender congruity. The Harry Benjamin International Gender Dysphoria Association has done much recently to develop standards of care; through its professional membership it has gone a long way in providing reliable information and references to persons who may be possible candidates for gender congruity. In years past, there were no standards of care. Scant attention was paid to psychological preparation prior to surgery, in many cases, and a number of persons who were licensed to practice medicine would perform genital surgery simply on the basis of patients paying the medical fees. These surgeons paid no attention to whether the patients had received hormone therapy, or if any of them ever had any cross-living experience; whether individuals were capable of coping in opposite gender roles or were actually transsexuals caused little concern to those surgeons. It is still possible to literally buy genital surgery without proper evaluation, counseling, and psychological and medical preparation, but this perversion of the gender congruity process is becoming less frequent as more providers become professional in their approaches to the problem and more reliable knowledge is made available to the medical and behavioral science communities as well as to the general public. This is in no small part due to the ethical standards developed by members of the Harry Benjamin International Gender Dysphoria Association. This organization holds a meeting every other year where workshops and seminars are conducted and professionals from all areas of the gender community make presentations. Physicians, surgeons, psychiatrists, psychologists, therapists, researchers, and many others gather from all over the world to attend these meetings. Not only does this allow them to share information (i.e., about the latest surgical techniques, the results of scientific research, etc.), but it also gives them an opportunity to meet each other and form professional relationships which often are continued beyond those meetings. In this manner, information is shared and spread at a continually accelerating pace. From what I have learned about this organization, and judging by the individuals I have met who are members, I have to give it very high marks for its goals and effectiveness. The Standards of Care adopted by the membership seem quite realistic, on balance. In reviewing them, there seem to be a few ambiguities, but the membeship recognized that some standards did need to be developed, and they had to have a beginning. They acknowledged that weaknesses and shortcomings might be incorporated into the initial revised draft, but they state quite clearly that suggestions for revisions or additions and deletions would be carefully considered in the future. All this seems quite reasonable and a very sensible approach. At least there are now standards of care; prior to their adoption, there were none.

Many of the present standards of care were practiced by responsible physicians, therapists, and surgeons before they were adopted by the Harry Benjamin International Gender Dysphoria Association. All too often, however, reasonable care was not given, and the results have been tragic. The case of Helen, the woman I discussed in Chapter 2, is an excellent example, but there are many others. An article recently appeared in a local southern California newspaper concerning one such case. It was a story about a female-to-male transsexual who was now attempting to return to his original female gender role after living as a man for well over ten years. I do not need to refer to the article, because I interviewed this man. His name is Ken. When I interviewed Ken, he brought numerous copies of newspaper articles with him, complete with pictures detailing problems he had encountered in obtaining proper treatment for his young son (Ken is the natural mother). The boy had developed a progressive disease of one of his vital organs. Ken gave me all of these articles, and they are still in my files.

Ken is the natural mother of three children. He has a long history of alcoholism, and there is a history of alcoholism on both sides of his family. Well over ten years ago Ken had a bilateral mastectomy, although he had not had any hormone therapy, psychological screening, or counseling, nor had he ever cross-lived. Several years later, and just a few months after he had given birth to his youngest child, he had a com- 113 plete hysterectomy, and his vagina was surgically closed. Ken had been receiving some therapy prior to these procedures, but he readily admitted to me that he had made the decision to have these surgeries performed while in an alcoholic haze.

In the article which said that he now wished to return to his original female gender role, Ken was quoted to the effect that what he had been doing for the last ten years or so — living as a man — was simply a masquerade on his part and a sick way to live out a long-standing fantasy. He indicated that he was going public with the interview to warn others who wanted to "change their sex" that it was not possible to do so. It is interesting to note, in any event, that later in the article he is quoted to the effect that he had volunteered himself for doctors to experiment on in order to try and provide him with his original sexual characteristics which had been surgically obliterated.

Whether Ken is a true transsexual is really not the important issue in this tragic story. Ken, an active alcoholic, was allowed to prescribe surgical procedures for himself without proper evaluation or social preparation. Based on what he told me in the interview, he was a very confused person, not only in terms of his gender, but his sexuality as well. He was tortured by guilt about what he had done and the consequences he had paid socially and in terms of rejection by his oldest child. Several years ago, and long after his surgical procedures, Ken unsuccessfully attempted to take his own life. He says at the present time that he is a recovering alcoholic, but his life has been left in shambles stemming from decisions hastily made in alcoholic stupors and surgery by a few irresponsible members of the medical community. Most certainly Ken has paid a dreadful price for his mistakes, but those mistakes would not have occurred had he been provided with responsible care and treatment to begin with. The sad part is that only Ken has to deal with the consequences of this irresponsibility.

On February 15, 1981, a story appeared in the San Francisco Chronicle, and was headlined: "TRANSSEXUAL WINS HER CASE, BUT IT'S TOO LATE." The story concerned a genetic male, Karl, who had been married. He had, quoting from the article, ". . .a history of psychiatric counseling going back to high school. He characterized his problems as 'severe gender identity confusion'." . . . Karl went to a number of doctors and therapy groups, and many of them indicated that he was a transsexual. Someone suggested he see a surgeon in

San Francisco, California, Dr. John Brown, who allegedly took advantage of his unstable condition. Mr. Brown had his medical license revoked by the State of California Board of Medical Quality Assurance in 1977. When last heard of, he was in another country. The story is further complicated by the fact that since Karl was not certain that he was a transsexual, he had specimens of his sperm placed in a sperm bank to provide his wife with the option of having children at a later date, if she so desired; Karl was a college student at the time. He then went to Dr. Brown (prior to 1977) and had genital surgery. Sometime after the surgery the sperm bank went bankrupt and notified Karl and his wife that his sperm had been rendered useless from heat. The San Francisco Chronicle story described a lawsuit Karl had brought against the now defunct sperm bank and the person who had allegedly originated the company. Karl was quoted as saying . . . "I consider myself a man. I always have. " . . . At another point in the story he was quoted as follows: . . . "I'm in limbo now, sexually. "

Unlike Helen in Chapter 2, Karl is living in a male gender role. But he is far from being a male sexually. Since he is living in a male role and thinks of himself as a male, he is, for all practical purposes, a eunuch.

Stories such as these should leave no doubt in anyone's mind that the Standards of Care developed by the Harry Benjamin International Gender Dysphoria Association have the welfare of people in mind. Many transsexuals with whom I talked felt that the Standards of Care only served to protect professional providers from liability. While they may possibly lend some protection to these professionals, I frankly see nothing wrong with that, particularly when these guidelines have been observed. But if those standards can prevent just one tragedy from occurring, just one less sensational headline, one less Helen, one less Ken, or one less Karl, the possibility that there is, in part, a self-serving motivation behind those standards does not trouble me in the least. I spent several hours with both Helen and Ken, and I feel real sorrow for them. Ken told me after the interview that in cases where people have young children and want to make a change, he might have to say to them: "It might not be worth the hell you have to go through." It most certainly is not worth the hell anyone would have to go through if he or she did not receive proper evaluation and counseling. There is no real turning back once surgery has been performed, and the emotional wounds can be far more painful to endure than the physical ones when mistakes are made.

A few former transsexuals have capitalized on the publicity they received due to pursuing gender congruity. They charge fees for speaking engagements with clubs, organizations on university campuses, and other groups interested in hearing about their lives and the subject of transsexualism. I suppose one would have to term them "professional transsexuals." Many former transsexuals have written autobiographical books about their lives or had them written for them by professional writers. The last thing most former transsexuals want is to call attention to themselves and make public appearances. Most transsexuals who make successful transitions disappear and just blend in with the rest of society. This is the primary reason it is so difficult for researchers to conduct follow-up studies on former transsexuals. Some former transsexuals who continue to make public appearances did not seek out publicity in the beginning; however, some did by writing autobiographies. They perhaps felt they had interesting stories to tell which would help to educate readers and went public with their stories out of real concern for others facing the same dilemmas. It is difficult to ascribe motives to others, and when we do we really perform a disservice. Whatever reasons some former transsexuals have had to make their lives public knowledge, they all have contributed to a better understanding of the subject of gender discomfort and the feelings involved.

Some former transsexuals, for any of a number of reasons, cannot seem to make adjustments after surgery, and continue to identify themselves as transsexuals. They just do not seem to be able to make that final transition of leaving the male world, and living in the female world, or being female, then living their lives as males. For whatever reasons, they remain transgendered emotionally and never fulfill their desires to be men or women. Sometimes guilt may be a factor; pressure from family rejection can stand in the way; unresolved emotional problems also may be a factor. If transsexuals have not prepared themselves emotionally prior to surgery to live in other gender roles, they are going to have great difficulty doing so after surgery. That is why the cross-role living experience is considered so important for preoperative surgical candidates. Cross-role living is not intended to have persons pretend to live in other roles and, perhaps, retreat back to more familiar roles when the going gets tough. Its purpose is to have them live full–time in gender roles opposite to those they were raised in. It is quite impossible for individuals to gauge whether they will be content living in opposite gender roles for the rest of their lives unless they actually have these experiences in realistic settings. Someone who goes to work as a woman, then lives a social life as a man, has no real conception of how she will function in the male role occupationally. Those who do this sort of thing are only playing "pretend" and, if they obtain surgery with such limited experience, they are very likely to fail in their efforts. Helen, Karl, and Ken are prime examples of what can happen to people when this key element of pursuing gender congruity is not observed. Even then there is a certain amount of risk, and no one can provide positive guarantees.

Many years ago I read a book, the title of which I have forgotten, about a white man who took a chemical to darken his skin pigment so that he could pass as a black and explore what it is like to be black in America. It was a very interesting book, but I felt the one weakness of his experiment was that if he desired, he could stop taking the medication and go back to the white world. He was not locked in, so to speak. Even though he had passed as a black, he had an escape hatch which blacks do not have. Psychologically, then, he could only partly experience what it was like to be black. Certainly there is a good analogy here. People can get a pretty good idea of what it is like to be considered male or female through cross-role living; but they have an escape route, and that is a little different from being locked into the roles through surgery. If any doubts should arise from cross-role living, they should be dealt with forthrightly before surgery.

Many transsexuals and would-be transsexuals have very naive and often hostile attitudes toward the public for not understanding their dilemmas, and toward the medical and mental health professions because of the rigorous requirements they have established in order for persons to pursue gender congruity. While conducting research for this book, I was invited to attend a transsexual-transvestite rap group to hear a speaker who is a well-known authority of the subject of gender identity. I was amazed to hear so many belligerent and antagonistic questions and comments. The air virtually crackled with hostility. As I conducted my interviews, I came across a great deal of that same hostility toward the public and the system. Many of the resentments transsexuals and would-be transsexuals have seem fully justified when put in perspective, but those who approach the system with chips on their shoulders are simply conducting exercises in futility. 117

When I asked the question, "Are you satisfied with the services that are presently available to help transsexuals?", eighty-four percent answered "no". I asked what faults they found, and numerous failings were related to me. I have placed them into seven general catagories: 1. A lack of communication of information; 2. Ignorance within the professional gender field, the medical field, and with the public; 3. Inadequate surgery; 4. Not enough services available (too thin); 5. The financial burden; 6. The whole system is too inflexible; 7. Transsexuals are not treated the same way other patients are treated. They are discriminated against.

I think it might be useful to examine these complaints and see what lies behind them. I pointed out at the very beginning of Chapter 7 that there seemed to be a glaring lack of information from readily accessible sources. There is no question in my mind this is a valid complaint, and the lack of information costs people time and money and often results in much frustration.

Depending on how one were to define "professional gender field," I might have to take exception to the first part of this second complaint, but only in part. Most of the professionals with whom I have come in contact are anything but ignorant. They are very much in tune with the problems transsexuals face and how they may best be helped. I cannot necessarily subscribe to each and every one of their methods but, in general, I have found them to be very knowledgeable and competent; but some professionals who have provided services for persons with gender problems have certainly given totally irresponsible treatment.

The charge that there is ignorance in the medical profession (including the mental health professions) and the general public is, I feel, a very valid comment. This book was written primarily to help the public better understand a condition most know little about but which has received widespread publicity. The fact that many professionals have little or no experience in the field of gender identity and are ignorant on the subject was well-documented by my interviews. At least half of the transsexuals I interviewed received treatment from physicians and therapists who had no knowledge of gender dysphoria. Many of them received ongoing therapy from professional therapists who admitted that they had no knowledge or experience related to gender discomfort. Some were supportive and willing to learn, according to those transsexuals I interviewed. In effect, the patients were paying fees to help educate therapists. Many transsexuals were treated by physicians who prescribed hormones for them. Barbara, a male-to-female transsexual, sought help from a psychiatrist in a large, midwestern city. The psychiatrist told her she was a homosexual and prescribed male sex hormones to make her feel more masculine. Judy, another male-to-female transsexual, went to a psychiatrist in New York who told her he would only treat her if she would try to learn to be a man. Abe, a female-to-male transsexual, was taken to his family physician by his mother when he was ten years old and prepubescent because of his persistent tomboy behavior. The doctor prescribed female hormones for Abe, and he immediately went into early puberty, developed pubic hair, large breasts, and started to menstruate. Sally was taken by her parents to a physician for a condition called hypospadia. The urethra exited the penis at its base. The doctor told Sally she was a hermaphrodite, and Sally assumed that was what had been causing her feelings of wanting to be a girl. Hypospadia is a genetic birth defect which has nothing to do with hermaphroditism, let alone how persons identify in the male gender role. To this day, Sally is convinced she is a transsexual because of her hypospadiac condition, even though it was surgically corrected.

All in all, members of the medical and mental health professions who have no knowledge of gender dysphoria have left many physical and emotional scars on persons troubled with gender confusion and gender discomfort. The mischief they have caused has very little basis on which it can be excused. The type of treatment Barbara, Judy, Abe, Sally, and many others have received is outrageous, and thoroughly unprofessional. The sad part is that treatment has been initiated, in many cases, on the basis of personal beliefs rather than sound medical practice. Those who find treatment of certain conditions repugnant to themselves or beyond their scope of knowledge should refer patients to professionals who are knowledgeable in those fields.

The adequacy of surgery is discussed in some detail in Chapter 8, and need not be covered again in this chapter.

The criticism that services for transsexuals are inadequate has some validity. Persons with gender discomfort usually have to move to large cities in order to obtain services. There are very few professionals who are skilled in treating transsexuals medically, psychologically, and surgically. It must be remembered, however, that other rare conditions have few specialists to treat them, and patients with those conditions or diseases have to go where the specialists are. Most physicians, psychologists, and psychiatrists will not come across a transsexual during the entire spans of their careers. The condition is that rare. In no way do I mean to imply that those in the medical and mental health fields should not be aware of gender dysphoria as a genuine condition; indeed, they should, and they also should have enough knowledge to be able to refer persons to clinics or specialists who provide professional treatment for gender dysphoria. Transsexualism is a recognized condition which causes much suffering for those who experience it and simply ignoring it will not make it go away.

Complaints about the financial burden of pursuing gender congruity are more than justified. The costs of treatment for gender discomfort are burdensome beyond belief. Hair removal for male–to–female transsexuals can run into the thousands of dollars. Psychotherapeutic treatment is very costly these days, as we all know. Genital surgery and ancillary cosmetic surgery can cost many thousands of dollars. Multiple surgeries for female-to-male transsexuals can range in the tens of thousands of dollars, and all of these costs continue to escalate. Obviously these kinds of sums are just not available to most people, and many who should have gender congruity surgery never receive it because of the financial constraints. Few insurance companies will cover the costs of gender congruity treatment, and this is true of Medicaid as well. Whether or not gender congruity treatment is necessary or not should not be left to the idiosyncratic judgments of insurance company executives or governmental bureaucrats. Professionals in the field of gender identity indicate that social, emotional, and hormonal rehabilitation followed by genital surgery is the treament indicated for some persons, and their judgments should be followed just as they are in other areas of medical and mental health.

Many transsexuals felt the whole system was too inflexible when it comes to the treatment of transsexuals. My personal observation is that the Harry Benjamin International Gender Dysphoria Association's Standards of Care are reasonable and not overly conservative. It must be remembered, however, that many clinics and specialists go well beyond the Standards of Care, which were designed to be minimum guidelines. Some gender clinics require an arbitrary two or three years of cross-role living prior to gender surgery. I think a minimum of one year is advisable but, beyond that, I do feel there should be more flexibility. Some transsexuals adapt very quickly to cross-role living, while others encounter countless

120

difficulties and do not adjust easily. It seems to me that a minimum of one year should be mandatory but, beyond that, decisions concerning surgery should be made on the basis of individual adjustment. It seems rather arbitrary to withold approval for surgery based on inflexible rules after a period of one year. In most cases, it seems to me, it should be evident within a year or so whether persons are going to be content and successfully live in other gender roles.

That transsexuals are discriminated against is indisputable. I have discussed that discrimination throughout this book. By and large, persons seeking help for gender discomfort have some very legitimate complaints concerning the system they are forced to deal with. Open, hostile confrontation, however, simply serves to put others on the defensive and seldom achieves any positive results. The civil rights movement of the nineteen sixties was based on peaceful protest and non-violent confrontation demanding equality. The results should have brought to the attention of all Americans that the system, cumbersome though it is, does work, and changes can be effected without destroying the system.

One attitude which pretty much pervades the male to female transsexual population is the desire to have large breasts. Unfortunately, we live in a very breast oriented culture, and bigger is considered better by many. These are absurd values, of course, but this emphasis does influence the thinking and feelings that genetic females have, as well as those male to female transsexuals have. Most male-to-female transsexuals are more insecure about their femininity than the average woman. Frequently, estrogenic hormones will provide male to-female transsexuals with small, but round and firm breasts. This happens to be the situation many genetic females are confronted with, and a large number of women have almost no breast development. "Cheaters," padded bras, breast prostheses, and breast augmentation surgery are big business in this country. Any physician who sees female patients on a daily basis knows that there are a great many women whose breasts are not nearly as large as they appear to be.

Large breasts are a fairly high priority for many male-to female transsexuals. One can hardly fault them, given our cultural values and their own insecurities concerning their femininity. I again must point out, however, that many women do not have breasts which are as large as they appear, and there are countless numbers of men — women as well, in the case of lesbians — who do not find large breasts at all attractive. I have met many men who have told me, quite honestly, that large breasts turn them off; they much prefer women who have small but, to them, attractive busts. Certainly if male-to-female transsexuals feel it is important to their internal body image, they should try to arrange breast augmentation surgery. I would only remind any woman considering this surgery that beauty is in the eye of the beholder, and not everybody appreciates large busts. I hope the day does come when both men and women realize we place far too much emphasis on the size of women's breasts and so little on the scope of their personalities and abilities. When that day arrives, we will have reached some degree of maturity as a culture. The essence of womanhood should not be measured by the cup sizes of women's bras.

Whether surgery is the proper treatment for some cases of gender dysphoria has been a controversy since modern genital surgery was first performed in the early nineteen fifties. Some behavioral scientists and physicians are totally opposed to surgery to resolve gender discomfort. They believe that psychiatric care is the proper treatment mode for transsexuals. Their positions were greatly enhanced with the publication of what is commonly referred to as the Meyer Report (Meyer and Reter, Johns Hopkins University, 1979). When that report was issued, John K. Meyer, M.D. was a psychiatrist on the staff at the Johns Hopkins Medical School. That university, of course, is where the first male to female gender congruity surgery took place in this country. The Meyer Report was the basis on which gender congruity surgery was discontinued at Johns Hopkins University, although many of Dr. Meyer's colleagues believed that the surgery should be continued. I have been told that Dr. Meyer has always been an opponent of surgical intervention to treat gender dysphoria and has advocated psychiatric treatment as the treatment of preference.

The Meyer Report received widespread attention in the press as well as in the medical and mental health professions. The report evaluated fifty applicants for gender congruity surgery at Johns Hopkins Gender Identity Clinic. A comparison was made between one group of fifteen persons who received surgery there, and thirty-five other applicants who did not complete the year of cross-role living; hence, they did not receive the surgery there (some later went on to have surgery elsewhere). The comparisons were made on the basis of job and educational stability and progress, stability in terms of marital relationships, and how many times persons in each group had moved. The Meyer Report concluded that since the group which was operated on did not show any significantly higher scores than the group which did not receive surgery, and some of the persons in the non-operated group improved their situations within the confines of his criteria, gential surgery was not justified. The criteria used by Dr. Meyer are socioeconomic, and I can understand how such a study might prove of some use if a group of persons of equal intelligence had received four years of college and was compared with a similar group who had no college education. What these criteria have to do with whether gender discomfort was relieved, I cannot even imagine. Although transsexualism can seriously affect socioeconomic conditions in persons' lives, it is a condition which only can be corrected by psychological and hormonal rehabilitation and surgical intervention. Perhaps the Meyer Report might have had some significance if the two groups compared were all persons qualified for surgery, but surgery was only performed for one group. Even then there would be gross statistical distortion, because the group not allowed to have surgery, in the name of scientific investigation would naturally feel frustrated and depressed, and their situations might well affect their socioeconomic circumstances. In point of fact, denial of surgery might well cause some to take their own lives. Since the unoperated group Dr. Meyer measured did not complete the year of cross-living, it is difficult if not impossible to tell whether members of that group were even transsexuals. The fact that they did not complete the year of cross-living is significant, because the only way professionals have of judging whether persons are truly transsexuals is for them to cross live for a significant period of time. If, at the end of that period of time, they have adjusted to the roles, express contentment in the roles and a desire to remain in the roles, they certainly have to be considered transsexuals and candidates for surgery. There are no physical or psychological tests to diagnose transsexualism, and that is why the practical cross living experience is so important to prevent people from making irreversible mistakes. Since the Meyer Report came out of such a prestigious university, it has had an undeniable impact, regardless of its validity. Other studies have come up with quite different results.

In 1981, Ira B. Pauly, M.D. published the results of research he had completed in the Australian and New Zealand Journal of Psychiatry. The report was titled, "Outcome of

Sex Reassignment Surgery for Transsexuals" [(1981) 15:45-51]. Dr. Pauly is a licensed psychiatrist and Diplomate, American Board of Neurology and Psychiatry. At the time of publication of the article, he was serving as professor and chairman: Department of Psychiatry and Behavioral Sciences, University of Nevada, Reno School of Medical Sciences, Reno, Nevada. He is the author of over a dozen papers on the subject of gender identity and transsexualism. Dr. Pauly's article described the results he obtained from his independent evaluation of several follow-up evaluations on gender reassigned, transsexual patients. His independent study of follow-up evaluations was comprised of two hundred and eighty three male-to-female transsexuals, and eighty-three female-to male transsexuals who underwent sex reassignment, hormone treatment, and/or surgery. The follow-up evaluations Dr. Pauly studied originated in Europe and the United States. They ranged in duration from less than one year to as long as nineteen years. His independent study indicated that just over seventy-one percent of the male-to-female transsexuals made satisfactory transitions, data was uncertain in seventeen percent of the cases, and just over two percent committed suicide. In the female-to-male group, Dr. Pauly found that over eighty percent made satisfactory transitions, six percent made unsatisfactory transitions, and data was uncertain in just over six percent of the cases.

It should be kept in mind that the process of gender congruity is a rehabilitative one, and it is not considered a cure. Persons are rehabilitated through hormone therapy, counseling, cross-gender living and, finally, surgical intervention. Transsexuals are not suddenly turned into men or women through surgery. It is a long and arduous process, and the prognosis is only favorable when all these conditions have been met. Dr. Paul Walker had this to say about the process: "Any person applying for sex reassignment surgery should receive very careful psychological evaluation and counseling. Many people can be helped by such counseling and sex reassignment surgery is not indicated in most cases. However, once a person has lived fulltime (at least one year), has been socially rehabilitated in part, reports happiness in the new sex role, and still wishes sex reassignment surgery (hormone therapy having been given during this period of time) sex reassignment surgery is now indicated and is mandatory. Such persons, after living at least one year in the new sex role, are firmly and irreversibly established in the social role of the new sex. That social role, if successful, validates and confirms their claim to be a psychologic member of the other sex. Sex reassignment is, therefore, mandatory to conform their anatomy to their social and psychologic sex.

"There are no reported cases in the world literature of a reversal of gender role and identity after a person has spent one year in the new sex role consistently and happily. To deny sex reassignment surgery at that point would condemn the person to a life of extremely poor body image, psychiatric disability, and potential suicide and/or severe depression."

The suicide rate among persons with gender discomfort is discouragingly high. In the group of persons I interviewed, twenty percent had attempted suicide at one point in their lives. Put another way, one out of every five persons I interviewed had tried to take his or her own life. I asked a question in my interview which is quite pertinent to this subject. The question was: "Suppose, for a moment, there were no such word as 'transsexualism' and no treatment for the condition, surgical or otherwise. How would you deal with the rest of your life?" Over one third answered that they would have eventually destroyed themselves emotionally or committed overt suicide. Almost sixteen percent said that they would have been very lonely and unhappy. These figures lend credence to Dr. Walker's statement describing what would happen to persons who had properly rehabilitated themselves and then had surgery denied to them.

Ironically, all former transsexuals are faced with another dilemma. Even though they may successfully pass rather close scrutiny, they know their backgrounds, and whether they should tell persons they may become intimate with usually becomes an issue. At this time, this is a question more former male-to-female transsexuals are concerned with than are former female-to-male transsexuals. Most female-to-male surgeries are not perfected to the point where those men can escape detection by their partners. They have no choice in most cases. This is not true, however, of former male-to-female transsexuals.

Most of the male-to-female transsexuals I spoke with indicated that they would tell partners they became intimate with about their backgrounds, if the relationships became serious. A few, however, stated that they would never tell partners, even if they were married. Hiding such a condition, in most states, would be considered contractual fraud and grounds for annulment. Fraud can be committed by an act of omission and does not have to be an overt act or lie.

At the least, this deception would have to be considered moral fraud of the worst sort. I do not feel anyone has the right to hide a transsexual background from a potential spouse, and this kind of deceit is the worst possible platform on which to begin a marital relationship that I can think of. It not only is totally unfair to future spouses, but it creates its own kind of hell. I know of two former male-to-female transsexuals who have married since their surgery, but have not told their husbands about their backgrounds. In effect, they have traded one lie for another. If the purpose of gender congruity is to relieve gender discomfort and throw off the yoke of pretense many transsexuals have lived with for so many years, it seems utterly senseless to put on another confining collar by employing this kind of deception. Both of the women I speak of live in constant fear that their husbands will discover their secrets and abandon them; and just what kind of life is that?

These are my personal, moral beliefs, of course, and each person must make an independent decision regarding this matter. The burden of the past is one of the realities all former transsexuals have to live with, however, and it seems almost certain that a relationship commenced with such willful deceit is very likely to fail. It just seems unconscionable to me to subject persons for whom love is professed to the likelihood of such terrible shock and pain.

Many former transsexuals were married in their biological gender roles. Some might ask if they were not committing the same type of fraud when they married in those roles. I do not think this is the case. Many of those persons married in the hope that marriage and possibly a family would relieve their gender discomfort, and there was no willful intent to deceive. Many of them made sincere efforts to live normal lives in their biological gender roles. Many did not even realize that they were transsexuals. No such innocence is present in the case of former transsexuals, however, and any deceit on their part is not only willful but very selfish.

Obviously, former transsexuals are going to make these decisions quite independent of my personal beliefs. I pointed out earlier in this book that gender congruity does not change the basic character values that individuals have. I suspect that former transsexuals who were honest in their personal relationships prior to gender congruity will feel it is important to discuss their backgrounds with future mates. On the other hand, it is quite likely that others who were not particularly honest in their dealings with others in the past, will continue to be this way when it comes to future relationships.

Because of their situations, former transsexuals do have a more difficult time finding meaningful relationships. Many potential partners will back off if they learn that persons they are starting to care about are former transsexuals. It takes a special kind of person who is secure in his own masculinity or her own femininity to understand these situations and love others for who they are, not what they may have been. Just because meaningful relationships are more difficult for former transsexuals to find, however, does not mean that there are not men and women in the world who can cope with these situations and not let this knowledge influence their feelings towards them. On the basis of what transsexuals have told me, I would have to say that there would seem to be no need for former transsexuals to talk about their backgrounds to everyone they come in contact with, but if intimate relationships are formed, former transsexuals would be better off in the long run, I should think, if they face up to the realities of their situations and not start serious relationships on a tissue of lies.

Persons who do follow the guidelines set up in the Standards of Care have a good chance for relief from gender discomfort through surgery. Lin Fraser, a therapist in San Francisco, California, has told me unequivocally that all persons she has worked with who have adhered to the Standards of Care and eventually had genital surgery have made successful adjustments in their new roles. Some of them may still have emotional problems they are working on, but the rehabilitative process combined with surgical intervention has relieved their gender discomfort. Gail was a pre-operative, male-to-female transsexual I interviewed. She has had surgery since I interviewed her, and she has kept in touch with me. Although she still has some problems to work out, she has no regrets about pursuing gender congruity. One day she told me she sometimes wonders what the compelling need was all about before surgery. The compelling need she spoke of was the tremendous drive she had to change her role due to a lifetime of gender discomfort. She described her feelings as being similar "to coming to a still pool of water after floating down a river of continuous rapids all my life." Gail, of course, faces the problems we all come across in life, and she has memories of having been raised and living in the male world which will remain with her for life. But the tension, the anxiety, and the emotional pain of having to live in an ill-fitting role are gone for her. That is what the process of gender congruity is all about, and nothing more can be expected from it. It does not solve extraneous problems, and it does not change persons' characters. Gail's analogy to still waters is a good one, and still waters, in terms of gender identity, are all that those suffering from gender discomfort can expect from the process of gender congruity.

# Chapter 11
# ANDROGYNY, MALE OR FEMALE?

With the advent of the beat generation of the nineteen fifties, followed by the flower children of the nineteen sixties, a new world was opened up which completely baffled older generations. Most persons, then and now, did not fully understand the significance of the changing attitudes these movements were signaling. Many misinterpreted the term "beat" and assumed it was intended to describe feelings of defeat and a desire by a whole generation to drop out of society. Beat was interpreted to mean beat down. In truth, the term "beat generation" did not spring from the verb to beat, which means to strike repeatedly. Beat generation was a media label, and was presented by the media in this light. The term beat came from the noun beatitude, which means a state of utmost bliss. This, of course, throws an entirely different light on the term beat generation. Not long after World War II, our western culture discovered eastern philosophy and religion. There was a tremendous surge of interest by young persons in eastern thought, particularly in America. As the nuclear family was slowly evolving, American youth, followed very quickly by young people in other western cultures, began to question some of the values their parents held dear. Many of these young people started to wonder whether there was more to life than simply earning a living, a home in the suburbs, and raising a family. As worldwide communications and travel became a reality, western and eastern cultures became more and more exposed to each other. Many young westerners turned to eastern philosophies and religions to look for answers to their philosophical queries about the meaning of life. Eastern approaches to life differ considerably from those in the west. Much more emphasis is placed on the self and feelings in eastern cultures than is so in western societies. Western philosophy has always tended to deal with the external rather than the internal. It also has been more of an exercise in Aristotelian logic than an examination of personal feelings and states of mind. Languages reflect those different approaches. Oriental languages have many words

129

and expressions describing feelings and states of mind. No words exist in occidental languages which are comparable, in many cases. Kipling's expression that "east is east and west is west, and never the twain shall meet" became obsolete in the nineteen fifties when a man by the name of Alan Watts appeared on the scene. Occasionally, someone comes along who seems capable of transcending cultures, and Alan Watts was such a man. He had the ability to put in western terms concepts totally alien to our culture. He had to use some linguistic gymnastics to achieve this purpose, but he was very adept at doing so. In Chapter 3 I used such words as "non-feeling" and "non-experience." Our language simply does not have words which express these concepts. Many words and expressions such as these became popularized, in no small part, thanks to Mr. Watts.

As young people began to grasp the significance of eastern approaches to life, many other things started to occur concurrently which have radically altered our society. The civil rights movement came into being; the sexual revolution took root, and the women's movement and feminism appeared on the scene. One of the results of all this social upheaval has been a trend toward androgyny. It was not very long after World War II that parents were grumbling that it was difficult to tell the boys from the girls, because they all wore pants and had long hair. In large measure, the trend toward androgyny got its start from an emphasis being placed on the self and a desire to explore and express the inner person. The pursuit of various forms of Asian meditation is commonplace now, and numerous westerners practice all sorts of eastern disciplines such as yoga and tai chi. With more energy being devoted to exploring the self, less emphasis was placed on stereotypical roles played so faithfully in previous generations. All the roles we played in society (breadwinner, sportsman, parent, etc.) were strongly influenced by our gender in the past. Men were supposed to support the family while women raised the children. Men were interested in active endeavors and women had more passive interests.

Circumstances have radically changed the composition of our society with respect to gender roles. A large percentage of the workforce is now made up of women, although most still earn much less than men. Many of these changes have been the result of the feminist movement, but some have occurred as a result of economic realities. It is difficult for most families to survive on a single paycheck anymore, and many women who might prefer to stay home have been forced to become financial contributors to their families. A large number of women also face the responsibility of providing for their children without financial assistance from men at all. On the other hand, many men are purposely involving themselves in the work of being parents, in the true sense of the word, to a much greater degree than in the past. Fifty years ago, our current way of life in America would have been considered science fiction. It is not difficult to understand why there has been a trend toward androgyny in our society as these changes have evolved. Many people vehemently condemn the blurring of gender roles which has come about in our society, while others praise the changes and feel they are long past due. Whether these changes are good or bad for society probably falls somewhere between these two viewpoints. I welcome many of the changes which have taken place in the last few generations. Many women have been forced to become more aware of economic realities, and considerable numbers of them have found great satisfaction and pleasure from participating at all levels of society. Some men have become much more flexible in their attitudes concerning the responsibilities they are willing to share in areas other than providing financial support. Some have realized that tenderness and emotional expression can be satisfying, masculine experiences. Changes of this sort are healthy and produce a more well-balanced society. On the other hand, some radical feminists would like to obliterate all gender roles. "Gender roles" has become a dirty phrase in some people's minds, but I cannot go along with that thinking. Our entire civilization is built on the cornerstones of roles people have played, and simply abandoning all traces of differences (other than obvious physiological ones) serves no useful purpose. It is akin to throwing the baby out with the bathwater.

The feminist movement became a reality in this country when women started to go out into the workforce in great numbers. They quickly discovered they not only were earning considerably less money than men, but they also had limited opportunities for advancement into higher paying jobs. Most of these conditions still exist today but to a slightly lesser degree. The women's movement has made real inroads in areas of legislation protecting women from sexual harassment and providing them with more opportunities than they had before. In the world of commerce and government, however, equality is still a goal, not a fact. The Legal Defense and Education Fund of the National Organization for Wo-  131 men recently published some figures which vividly illustrate this point. "Women college graduates are paid four hundred dollars a year less than men who have only finished elementary school" (United States Department of Labor, Women's Bureau – The Earnings Gap Between Women and Men, 1979). "More than eighty percent of all working women are crowded into clerical, service, sales and manufacturing jobs, where wages are significantly lower than male dominated manufacturing jobs and skilled trades" (Research Summary Series #4, Business and Professional Women's Foundation). "Even with advances in technology, working women are still being hurt. Recent changes have led to most computer programmer, keypunch and microassembly jobs being classified as 'women's work', with significant drops in pay" (Research Summary Series # 4, Business and Professional Women's Foundation). "Although three out of every four people eligible and registered in Federal work incentive programs are women, a statute requires unemployed fathers to be given priority in placement. When women are placed in jobs through this program, they earn an entry salary of two dollars and ninety-seven cents an hour — less than three-quarters of the man's four dollar and one cent per hour" (United States Commission on Civil Rights, Clearinghouse publication 68).

The types of discrimination cited by NOW, combined with the failure of the Equal Rights Amendment to achieve ratification, clearly indicate that our society has a long way to go before gender equality is a reality. However, the women's movement is alive and well, and pressure will continue to be brought on legislative bodies to provide equality under the law and the constitution, and pressure exerted on administrators, both governmental and private, to ensure that laws are administered on an equitable basis.

I consider myself a feminist, and believe the types of things I have been discussing are what feminism is all about. I have to part company with some radical feminists who would prefer to obliterate all differences between the genders, wherever possible. The goal of feminism should be *equality*, not *sameness*. Women can be provided with equal opportunity without forcing them to become pseudo-men. Men can learn to be tender, expressive of their emotions, and nurturing without abandoning their masculinity. These are human characteristics, and when we deny them to men, we deny them equality in terms of being human.

Equal opportunity goes far deeper, however, than simply advertising the slogan, "An equal opportunity employer".

Let me illustrate this point. For a long time, it has been said that girls are not as good at math and hard sciences as boys are. Most certainly if girls are told this as they matriculate and progress through school, myth becomes fact. Girls are very likely to *live down* to those expectations. Consider the following statement: "Sixty-five percent of teenage boys have had enough math to enroll in college calculus in this country — the gateway to science and technology careers — compared to forty-five percent of girls so prepared" (National Science Foundation, Directorate for Science Education, Science Datebook). Myth has become fact, yet it is not based on any hard evidence that boys are better at these subjects than girls. It is due to girls being discouraged from exploring these fields.

Feminism, because its goal is equality, has to embrace the concept of equality for men and women if we are to have a balanced society. Each and every child should have the opportunity to explore his or her potential to its limits and not become bogged down with gender roles stereotypes. These stereotypes stand as barriers to human development and should be done away with. Earlier in this book I discussed the differences in attitudes that boys and girls are brought up with concerning sexual activity. I pointed out that boys are usually raised to believe that sex, outside of a loving relationship, is perfectly acceptable for them, but girls are taught that sex is only acceptable within a loving relationship. Society has also discouraged boys from crying and expressing their emotions. We (society) give boys toys which teach them about the external world but discourage them from learning to be nurturing by playing with dolls. Suddenly, when they grow into young manhood, they are expected to establish families and become loving, caring, nurturing fathers and husbands. This expectation goes against the grain of a good deal they have been taught (or not taught) since they were infants. It seems to me this is expecting a great deal from young men, and it is not hard to understand why men and women frequently have great difficulty understanding the thinking and behavior of one another. Our divorce rate certainly reflects this sad fact. Equality should not be equated with sameness. There are always going to be differences between men and women and gender role characteristics, but we badly need to re-define gender roles in order to provide equality for men as well as women.

Gender identity is something most of us take very much for granted. We seldom think about it and just go about our lives in gender roles. Gender roles, however, serve as clear beacons to all of us, although we do not think about them often in this way. The total obliteration of gender role characteristics would, I feel, create serious disorientation (not to mention boredom), and I doubt that any society could function for long without them. "Well!", some would say. "Isn't that exactly what we do when people dress the same and often perform the same tasks?" My answer is that there is more than one way to define gender roles. If we define them in a constraining manner, so that individuals feel guilty for dressing in a manner even resembling the opposite gender or having thoughts, feelings, or mannerisms considered to belong exclusively to those of the opposite gender, we develop a society similar to the one we have been struggling to emerge from. In the past, we defined gender roles with such expressions as "he wears the pants in the family", "macho", "ladylike", and many other terms all stemming from a concept of dominance and power. We do not have to define gender roles in these terms unless we wish to do so. When we do, we repress both men and women. Men are precluded from crying and expressing their emotions, women are not allowed to exercise their minds and to achieve success based not on their beauty but their intellectual capacities. On the other hand, men and women have obvious physiological differences, and they will always have somewhat different natures. We can, however, re-define many of the stereotypes, if we so desire. It does not have to be considered unmasculine for a man to be tender or cry and express his emotions. It does not have to be considered unfeminine for a woman to fix a car, drive a truck, or be assertive. When we define gender roles in these ways, we encourage unnecessary constraints on humanity, and these types of constraints lead to a very unequal society. Men and women, if given the opportunity, will pursue various activities in our society which have little to do with gender differences. Men and women, on the other hand, are constituted quite differently reproductively and hormonally, and these differences are usually quite obvious. We really do not need a lot of very artificial stereotypes to clearly define the genders.

It has always interested me that we have been almost obsessive in our need to set up boundaries between manhood and womanhood. Our society has been very hard on persons who strayed beyond those arbitrary boundaries, and those who did not clearly define themselves as males or females were, and still are to a large extent, outcasts. In reality, we are all human beings, and men and women share that humanity. While there are very obvious physiological differences, men and women have much in common. They both produce male and female sex hormones, as well as numerous other chemicals. They have similar digestive systems and vital organs, and their bodily functions work pretty much the same way, with the exception of reproduction. Even there, all is not black and white. Modern science has destroyed an old and treasured myth that woman was created from the rib of man. When an egg is fertilized and starts its journey down the fallopian tube to attach itself to the uterus, that newly formed embryo is genetically programmed to become male or female. Physiologically, however, all embryos are potentially female until certain chemical-hormonal events occur in the first few weeks after conception. When events are genetically triggered, gonads, which are potential ovaries, descend in the inguinal region and develop into testes in the scrotum instead. If, for some reason, this chemical-hormonal process were not to occur in a genetically programmed male, the embryo would remain female, physiologically. In reality, we all start embryonic life as potential females, and embryos only develop into males if signals present in the chromosomes trigger certain events to occur. That, of course, is why all males have rudimentary nipples on their breasts. All embryonic life is potentially female until genetic determinants alter the course of events. Now, all this may cause strong men to weep, but it serves to illustrate how marvelously complex human life is and how much men and women really have in common. That should not make anyone sad, for it provides us with our common bond of humanity.

Since men and women have much in common biologically, and certainly intellectually, it is not surprising, given the vicissitudes of nature, that some individuals seem to come out somewhere between male and female. Some genuinely choose a middle ground, while others may be there because of gender confusion or, perhaps in some cases, hormonal imbalances. Whatever the reason, there are a number of people who would have to be characterized as androgynous in the context society defines masculine and feminine. This middle ground varies in degree from what is defined as "nearly masculine" to "nearly feminine" by those who would rate gender on a scale. Androgyny, as it applies to human beings, is defined as the state of having the characteristics of male and female, being both male and female. This term should be distinguished from hermaphroditism in humans, which is the state of being born with some or all of the reproductive organs of both sexes. Hermaphroditism refers to the sexual characteristics, particularly the primary ones. Androgyny describes the appearance and, often, the state of mind of persons. We all have seen persons who could easily be male or female. Sometimes the blend is so perfect that it simply is impossible to label them on the basis of their presentations. This is a state of true androgyny. As I noted, androgyny can also refer to persons' states of mind, and how they view themselves in terms of gender identity. Many relate to both genders, to some extent, and they frequently present this appearance to the public. Quite often they are rejecting gender role stereotypes, and feel quite comfortable in displaying their maleness and their femaleness at the same time. If they are comfortable in this situation, they are certainly entitled to their feelings and the life-styles they may choose. They are not necessarily confused and, if they are comfortable in those roles, they have to be considered mentally healthy. Simply because most of society does not approve of their appearances, and often their life-styles, is not an indication these persons have emotional problems. Like all other human beings, those who happen to be androgynous are also sexual beings, and I think that this is where the taboos dictate disapproval. Many of these individuals are bisexual, and bisexuality or homosexuality are long-standing taboos in this culture.

Other androgynous persons may not be comfortable with their states of mind, and may be searching for answers. Indeed, they may be transsexuals or transvestites. There are all gradations of intensity of androgyny, and the picture can become muddied very quickly when people do not have a clear understanding of what all this means. It is quite understandable that transvestism and transsexualism have become enmeshed in the morass of androgyny, because some transvestites and transsexuals do have very androgynous presentations. Logically, however, androgyny is not a link to either condition, although it is easy enough to fall into this linguist trap. Those who are androgynous may or may not be transvestites or transsexuals, but that does not give us a right to link them based on the elusive chain of androgyny.

There is a quite separate issue related to transsexualism and transvestism. I refer to what professionals in the gender field call "the continuum" or "gray area." These two terms are usually applied to persons who seem to be somewhere between true transvestism and true transsexualism. Ironically, Harry Benjamin, M.D., in his book, *The Transsexual Phenomenon\**, promoted the concept of a link or continuum between transvestism and transsexualism. He did this on the basis of his observation that some persons fall somewhere in between the two conditions. Dr. Benjamin used the folfowing labels: "psuedo-transvestite"; "fetishistic transvestite"; "true transvestite", "transsexual, non-surgical"; "transsexual, moderate intensity"; "transsexual, high intensity". He also presented a "Sex Orientation Scale" ("Sex and Gender Role Disorientation and Indecision"). In this scale, Dr. Benjamin listed several subjects such as "Gender 'Feeling' ", cross-dressing and social habits, sexual orientation, whether they should have psychotherapy, estrogen therapy, and genital surgery. He then rated the various catagories of transvestites and transsexuals that he had labeled on the basis of these subjects. For example, concerning the subject of cross dressing and social habits, he says, "True Transvestites": "Dresses constantly or as often as possible. May live and be accepted as a woman. May 'dress' underneath male clothes, if no other choice."

I have great respect for Dr. Benjamin and the pioneering work he did. His concern and compassion for those with gender or sexual problems is beyond dispute. I have to take exception with him and others, however, when such a scale is applied to two entirely different conditions. There is unquestionably a large group of persons who do seem to fall somewhere between transvestism and transsexualism. I see no value in rating scales with respect to transsexuals and transvestites. I firmly believe such a concept tends to cloud the issues, obfuscate terminology, and lead persons down the path of false logic. On page 27 of the soft-cover edition of his book, Dr. Benjamin makes the following statement: "These persons can somewhat appease their unhappiness by dressing in the clothes of the opposite sex, that is to say, by cross-dressing, and they are, therefore, transvestites too." In Chapter 2 I pointed out that this conclusion is a false syllogism and not a valid deduction. My purpose here is not to attack the work of Dr. Benjamin; far from it. I am trying to illustrate how easy it is to confuse issues by using incorrect logic. Although there is no question that many persons exist

*Warner Books, 1966

in states which are not easy to define as transvestism or trans-sexualism, the linking of the two by means of a scale is where the continuum originates, not from the facts. The persons who feel that transsexuals and transvestites should be rated on a scale have created a continuum by the very logic of their reasoning. The problem, as I see it, is that this reasoning does not have a basis in logic. There is no relationship between transvestism and transsexualism. They have one common behavior pattern, and that is cross-dressing. But some have parlayed that one common denominator, and the fact that sometimes transvestites and transsexuals have androgynous presentations, into a relationship between the two conditions which simply is non-existant. Others have rated individuals on a sexual orientation scale. Using a rating scale to measure degrees of sexual orientation, a single subject, provides consistency to what is being rated, but I cannot find that consistency in a scale which creates a link between transvestism and transsexualism. The link is in the eye of the creator, not in fact.

I discussed transvestism, transsexualism, sexual orientation, and sexuality in great detail in Chapter 2 of this book. Very briefly, I pointed out that transvestism is a clearly definable sexual condition which may or may not be affected by gender confusion. Transsexualism is a clearly definable gender condition which may or may not be accompanied by gender confusion or sexual conditions. Many transsexuals I interviewed told me they had been transvestites before they "became transsexuals" or they went through a "transvestic state." This is the very type of confusion which results due to fuzzy reasoning linking the two conditions by a continuum. By making such statements, these persons meant that they had thought of themselves as transvestites before they realized they were actually transsexuals, or they simply felt transvestism was a first step toward transsexualism. This simply is not so. Persons do not advance from transvestism to transsexualism. Because of gender confusion or other emotional problems, they may not realize they are transsexuals and just assume they are transvestites because they cross dress. Many persons who are transvestites mistakenly believe they are transsexuals because of their cross-dressing patterns, and their gender confusion.

If one were to use the dictionary definition (a transvestite is a person who adopts the dress, and often the behavior of the opposite sex), I suppose, in the very loosest sense, we could say that some transsexuals are also transvestites. I pointed out in Chapter 2, however, that the definition the dictionary provides us with is completely inadequate, and that incompleteness has greatly contributed to so many people — including some professionals — failing to clearly distinguish between two very different conditions. When we discuss two subjects which both involve sexuality and have similar behavior patterns, we have to be very precise in defining the terms. That same, very imprecise definition could be applied to transsexuals, but it would be just as meaningless in that context. I could define bears as mammals that are usually omniverous. I could also define humans in the same manner, and both definitions would be correct, but they tell us little about bears or humans — only some traits they have in common. Since transsexualism and transvestism often involve sexuality and cross-dressing patterns, we have to be very explicit when discussing them. The salient difference between the two conditions is that transsexualism arises from very painful emotional discomfort concerning individuals' gender roles, and often begins in the earliest stages of self-awareness — anywhere from eighteen months to four or five years of age. Transvestism arises from completely different issues, and although they have similar behavior patterns (cross-dressing), in some cases, the root causes are totally dissimilar, as are the resolution of any problems the conditions may cause. In many cases, the only problems which arise for transvestites are feelings of guilt, and those feelings can usually be dealt with through conventional psychotherapy. Unfortunately, that is not the case for transsexuals, because psychotherapy does not relieve gender role discomfort.

A social factor often plays a part in the confusion between transsexualism and transvestism. There is peer pressure in the gender community. Frequently, transsexuals and transvestites meet together in rap groups. Some very interesting group dynamics come into play when the two groups mix. Transvestism is a sexual condition, but according to Lin Fraser, behavior patterns such as cross-dressing can be modified by heterosexual transvestites with psychotherapeutic help. Behavior patterns in transsexuals are considered beyond the control of transsexuals, however. Therefore, transsexualism is considered a more acceptable condition, because transsexuals cannot control their feelings. Many transvestites are prompted to label themselves as transsexuals and thereby avoid responsibility for their feelings and behavior. It is also

139

interesting to note that male-to-female transsexuals are changing from what has been traditionally thought of as the superior gender to the "weaker sex" (gender). Since transsexuals supposedly have no control over their feelings, transvestites can avoid the stigma of voluntarily behaving like the "weaker sex" by labeling themselves transsexuals.

To perpetuate the concept of a continuum between the conditions of transsexualism and transvestism simply creates more barriers for those who are trying to understand their sexuality and their gender identity. That there seem to be varying degrees of intensity of both transsexualism and transvestism is an observable fact, but to draw an imaginary line between the two and call it a continuum only confuses the issues. As human beings we are finite, so it is difficult for us to cope with concepts such as infinity. We tend to want to set up beginnings and endings; that way we can account for what is in between. In the case of transsexualism or transvestism, there is no need to draw a line between the two conditions to explain what seems to be neither one or the other. The fact that many of these persons who are difficult to define are often androgynous further complicates the issues. All of these conditions are complex and overlayed with a patina of myth, because they all concern sexuality to some degree; and there are no subjects which are surrounded by as many cultural taboos and myths as sexuality and gender role behavior. Fuzzy thinking not only can create myths, but it can establish real obstacles to separating myth from fact. Truth is never easy to come by, and when subjects are obscured by social taboos, it is doubly difficult to examine them when the myths are perpetuated by muddled reasoning.

We are a society which functions on information, and information is often reduced to scales, graphs, and statistical charts. I feel we make a great mistake when we attempt to reduce the complexities of human feelings to these forms. Certainly statistical data can be useful when studying human sexual activity, for example, but those statistics cannot probe the human mind and all its complexities. Statistics are really only as good as their interpretation anyway, and when we ascribe human motivation to empirical evidence, we tread on very shaky ground. It is very easy to apply false logic to statistical information, and it frequently leads us down blind trails. If I say that oranges are round and that they are fruit, I have stated two facts. However, supposing I also say baseballs are round. Am I then justified in concluding that they are fruit? Of course not; but this same type of false logic is sometimes used in statistical interpretation, sometimes innocently, sometimes with purpose of mind. If I have a product to sell, or a point of view to put across, it probably is in my best interest to present empirical data in a manner which will sell my product or my point of view. Whether I present false conclusions in statistical form through innocence and a desire to sell my product or point of view, or by design, people are going to be misled. I think much the same thing has happened in relation to efforts made to understand human sexuality and gender identity. The whole area is complex beyond belief, and persons have studied individual aspects, letting their observations color their thinking regarding other areas of these same subjects. All too often, theory and analysis commenced in one area influence theory and analysis in other areas where they may have no basis in fact. Eventually, the whole subject becomes a quagmire which is impossible to wade through. Issues become blurred, and individual problems are approached from preconceived notions.

There are individuals who are difficult to label as transvestites or transsexuals. I do not dispute that for a moment. I do feel, however, it is a grave mistake to label this spectrum of persons as a continuum between transsexualism and transvestitism. Some in that gray area may indeed be transvestites or transsexuals. Conversely, they may be neither. I think we could logically call androgyny a continuum, but not a continuum between transsexualism and transvestism. It is a continuum between the genders. It illustrates various degrees of masculinity and feminity, as defined by society. It makes some sense to talk about a continuum in this respect, but it makes no sense to discuss a continuum between sexual conditions and gender conditions. When we do this, we create confusion and divert the attention of those attempting to understand very complex but quite different subjects. A gender scale or continuum might be quite helpful in measuring gradations of masculinity and feminity, but it is meaningless when applied to completely different subjects — one a gender condition, the other a sexual condition.

# Chapter 12
# SOME COMMON GROUND

When I was very young, my father often read stories or books to me before I went to sleep. He would sit on a chair next to my bed, and I would snuggle under the covers, close my eyes, and let my imagination become so active I would actually become part of a story and think of myself as one of the characters in the stories. I suppose this happens to all of us, to some extent, when we read books or stories or have them read to us. It is also why drama on the radio was referred to as "theater of the mind." Since we could not see the actors and only heard their voices, we had to conjure in our minds what the characters they were portraying looked like and what their mannerisms were. I have never found television viewing to be quite as much fun as listening to the radio when I was a child. Very little is left to the imagination in a television drama, and we become a much more passive audience. Radio drama and reading or being read to always let my imagination range much further.

One book my father read to me several times (at my insistence) was a book about a little girl and a secret she had. The story concerned a young girl who went to live with relatives on a large estate. There was an old ivy covered wall on the grounds which enclosed a world the little girl only could imagine. She watched as birds flew over the wall and envied their ability to see what she could not. One day, while exploring the outside of the wall, she found an old door hidden behind another wall of ivy and undergrowth. After much effort, she was able to get the door open and enter that mysterious enclosure. Behind those walls was the most beautiful garden she had ever seen. More flowers than she had ever imagined existed were everywhere, and lovely old trees provided shade and contrast. From that day on, the little girl would slip away through the door leading to her secret garden and explore the joys she would find there. The secret garden was her refuge from the drab world outside its walls.

It would be nice if the secrets transsexuals harbor as they are growing up were as pleasant as those in that little girl's secret garden. Unfortunately, their secrets often carry the sting of emotional pain, turmoil, and confusion. Most of the persons I talked to felt they were the only ones who had the feelings they had when they were young, and they felt very guilty for feeling the way they did. Although their fantasies sometimes brought them temporary pleasures and relief, the realities of the world decended upon them again soon enough. So often the feelings transsexuals experienced were more like struggling through cactus patches overgrown with briars and other thorny underbrush. It was anything but a garden of pleasure for those who experienced it.

Earlier in this book I mentioned that there is still much controversy about what causes the condition of transsexualism and that scientists had not been able to come up with any definitive answers to date. That is certainly a fact, but since transsexuals seem to tread such an uncomfortable path, usually starting very early in life, it seems to me it is worthwhile to at least examine some of the possibilities.

When the story of Christine Jorgensen first made headlines in the early 1950s, it was dubbed "sex change", and that label has stuck like glue to transsexuals. This label is totally inappropriate and misleading, as I have pointed out several times in this book. The implication of this term is that persons are men one moment, have surgery, and then become women; or that women have surgical procedures which turn them into instant men. Nothing could be further from the truth. Most changes which do occur happen long before surgery is ever considered. Individuals must cross-live in new gender roles for a minimum of one year in all aspects of their lives; only if they are successful in doing this and report they are happy in the new roles is surgery ever recommended. Surgery amounts to nothing more than some alterations of the sexual organs of transsexuals in order to allow sexual function in roles in which they have already been functioning in all other aspects of their lives. If they are male-to-female transsexuals, for instance, their hormonal chemistry has been altered to that of females. Those hormonal changes also induce some changes in their secondary sexual characteristics which are more typically female. If they work, they earn their livings as females, not males. They interact with people around them as females; with the exception of the sexual organs, they function as women. Surgery simply allows them to live their lives sexually in roles compatible with their personal gender identity. It also provides security through a sense of completeness as men or women. So much attention 143 has been given to the surgical aspects of transsexualism that little else has been considered by the media and the public.

Much speculation has arisen as to what might cause people to feel uncomfortable in their biological gender roles and wish to change them. Unfortunately, most of the speculation revolved around them changing their sexes, and I have already pointed out that this is a self-limiting phrase. Many psychiatrists believed the desire to change gender originated from upbringing. Some cling to this notion to this day, despite overwhelming evidence to the contrary. The favorite theory was, and still is in some minds, that the feelings which transsexuals experience are the result of domineering mothers raising children with fathers who were considered passive or absent altogether. In other words, they were suggesting that male-to-female transsexuals did not have strong, masculine father images. Accordingly, transsexuals were not able to shake off the feminine identity with their mothers, which most boys do, and develop masculine identities. The facts just do not support this conclusion. I found no evidence that such a link exists. The transsexuals I interviewed came from very diverse family backgrounds, and there was nothing to indicate that any link exists between their transsexual conditions and their family backgrounds. Of course this theory does not account at all for the existence of female-to-male transsexualism. Also, many of the transsexuals I interviewed were raised by mothers who were very passive, and had fathers who not only were aggressive but very much involved in decisions regarding the rearing of their children.

A number of people have asked me if transsexualism might be caused by one or both parents treating children more like their biological gender role opposites than their true biological gender. I did talk to a few persons where this was the case. Two boys had been encouraged to dress in girls' clothing by their mothers, and two female-to-male transsexuals whom I interviewed had been treated more like boys than girls by either one or both of their parents when they were growing up. They, however, were only four out of the more than seventy persons I interviewed. Conversely, many parents of persons I interveiwed went to some lengths to discourage children who exhibited opposite gender role behavior in any form. On the other hand, some parents simply ignored any such behavior. A large percentage of the persons I interviewed exhibited no cross-role behavior patterns, and their parents had no idea they harbored any but very normal feelings concerning their gender identities until they were told.

On balance, transsexuals seem to have their feelings of discomfort quite independent of their cultural or family backgrounds and upbringing.

If environment were the principle cause of transsexualism, we certainly would have to question why it seems totally immune to psychiatric reversal. Just about everything has been tried to change the feelings of transsexuals, with an overwhelming lack of success. The treatments which have been tried range from intense psychotherapy, electro-shock, immersion in totally masculine or feminine environments to hormone therapy. Nothing seems to have worked, and the failure rate is virtually one hundred percent. The problem with these types of approaches, as I see it, is that treatment has been aimed at altering behavioral manifestations which are based on feelings concerning core gender identity. It seems certain that should similar goals be set for non-transsexuals, the failure rate would be equally spectacular. Perhaps if it is put on a more personal level the reader will more fully appreciate the futility of these endeavors. If you are a man, how would you react if a psychiatrist, or anyone else, tried to convince you it was important for you to stop feeling like a man and feel like a woman? If you are a woman, what would be your response if an effort were made to persuade you to not feel like a woman, and you were told you should feel like a man? Both male and female readers would, I am sure, consider these efforts sheer insanity and no matter what anyone said or did, your conception of yourselves as males or females would not be altered. Changing people's feelings about their male or female identities is just not possible. This is just as true for transsexuals as it is for non-transsexuals. Although many transsexuals have considerable confusion about their gender identity, the confusion is based on the anomaly of having the body of one gender, while identifying with the opposite gender. Almost anyone would develop confusion and insecurity about his or her gender identity under those circumstances; the fact that some may have confusion, however, does not alter their basic feelings which usually have existed from their earliest memories. After listening to so many stories of lives being disrupted, families torn apart, and monstrous financial burdens, if there were any evidence that psychotherapy could help persons eliminate their feelings of gender discomfort, this writer would be the first in line to call for an end to rehabilitative treatment and surgery. I most certainly wish I could report this as fact, but there simply is not one iota of evidence that treatment has any lasting effect.

Since the core of gender identity seems to be so deeply rooted in all of us, we have to examine the possibility that transsexualism may spring, at least in part, from persons' genetic composition or some biological process. If genetic determinism were the only alternative to be considered in searching for the roots of transsexualism, however, environmental factors would have to be suspect, no matter how intractable the feelings. Genetic determinism, as a singular origin, is not the answer to what causes transsexualism. Ordinary females carry two chromosomes in all their cells which are genetically coded as female. Geneticists call these chromosomes XX. Ordinary men also carry two genetically coded chromosomes in their cells. One chormosome is X, but the other is labeled Y. Only normal, genetic males have the Y chromosomes in all their cells, and all normal genetic females only have X chromosomes. Approximately fifty percent of the male sperm carry only XX chromosomes, while the other fifty percent carry XY chromosomes. If a sperm carrying XY chromosomes should be the one to fertilize an egg, the embryo, genetically, would be destined to become male. If a sperm carrying only XX chromosomes should fertilize the egg, the embryo, genetically, would be destined to become female.

With rare exceptions, transsexuals who have been tested for chromosomes in their cells have been found to have a chromosomal compatability with their biological gender (specifically, having male or female reproductive organs). Therefore, most male-to-female transsexuals have XY chromosomes in all their cells, and most female-to-male transsexuals have only XX chromosomes in their cells. If chromosomal makeup were a determinant for causing transsexualism, one would expect to find many transsexuals whose chromosomal makeup were not compatible with their reproductive organs.

Chromosomal makeup of XX and XY determinants is not the complete story, however. All of us, women and men, have antigens in our bodies. Antigens are substances which are capable, under appropriate conditions, of inducing specific immune responses and of reacting with the products of those responses. There is an antigen found in the chromosomal male cellular structure, and even in male sperm, which is called ''The HY Antigen.'' It seems to be the substance which causes chromosomes to pass along the genetic triggers which determine if an embryo is to become male. Normal men are HY antigen positive, and normal women test as HY negative. In other words, normal males carry the HY antigens in the membranes of all their cells as well as in their sperm, and normal women do not have HY antigens in their cellular makeup. Some very interesting experiments have been conducted in West Germany by Wolf Eicher, Ph.D. and several of his colleagues. Some information regarding this research was reported in the letters to the editor column of The Lancet (The Lancet, November 24, 1979, 1137-1138), an English medical journal; Dr. Eicher also made a presentation on this same research at the Fourth World Congress of Sexology (December 16-21, 1979) in Mexico. Dr. Eicher and his colleagues studied a number of male-to-female and female-to male transsexuals whose chromosomal characteristics were compatible with their reproductive organs. The male-to-female transsexuals tested XY chromosomally, and the female to−male transsexuals XX chromosomally. In eight out of eleven male to female transsexuals tested, he found HY negative results, one tested intermediate (weak-positive), and two tested positive. In eleven female-to-male transsexuals tested, nine were HY positive, one was intermediate, and one was negative. This research, although it is small in numbers, certainly raises some questions concerning biological factors interrupting genetic determinants and whether present tests even provide us with conclusive information regarding genetic makeup. Many of the persons tested, however, had been undergoing hormone therapy, so it is not clear whether opposite gender sex hormones may have had an affect on HY antigen testings. More testing with stricter control of much larger groups is needed to establish scientific credibility, but this research offers the possibility of providing at least one of the unknown links which may influence the condition of transsexualism.

Little money has been available for research on the causes of transsexualism, most likely because the process of gender congruity has met with disapproval by the public and a large segment of the medical and mental health professions. Research in other areas, however, certainly has filled many of the gaps in our knowledge of genetics and chemical-hormonal influences. Genetic engineering is no longer a dream but a reality being put to practical, commercial uses. One of the more interesting pieces of research I came across was reported to the Endocrine Society at a meeting held in San Francisco,

California, June 17th and 18th, 1982. This society is comprised of specialists who study the various compounds produced in the glands of our bodies. The report was presented by Dr. Fernando Nottebohm of the Rockefeller University in New York. Dr. Nottebohm's research dealt with songbirds, and canaries were the subject of his experiments. With the knowledge that only male canaries sing, and they only sing during the mating season, Dr. Nottebohm treated female canaries with the male hormone, testosterone. The results were spectacular. When female canaries received this hormone, the nerve cells in their forebrains doubled to the approximate number found in male canaries, and these female canaries started singing like male canaries. Another interesting fact Dr. Nottebohm described was that when the mating season ends, the testosterone level in male canaries falls almost ninety percent and the number of nerve cells in their forebrains actually diminish. The males then stop singing until a new mating season arrives. At that time, their testosterone levels increase dramatically, as do the number of cells in their forebrains, and they start singing again.

Another report was presented at this same conference which I feel is even more significant, as it may relate to the condition of transsexualism. I quote from an article in the San Francisco Chronicle of Thursday, June 17, 1982, written by the Science Editor, David Perlman: ..."A similar hormonal influence on the growth of brain tissue in mammals was reported by Dr. Roger A. Gorski of the University of California at Los Angeles, who has been studying the tissues of rat brains for more than 20 years.

"There are major differences in brain function between male and female rats, Gorski told reporters, although, as in all other mammals, the brain starts out as 'basically female'.

"In other words, it takes the influence of male sex hormones to cause a newly forming animal brain to develop the characteristics that mark a male. As if to prove that point, Gorski's experiments have shown that when newborn male rats are castrated the lack of testicular hormones causes them to grow up behaving exactly like females. By contrast, Gorski said, a single dose of testosterone during a female rat's first week of life will permanently turn her brain into a 'masculine' one."

There is a great deal of research being conducted with respect to genetics and hormones and their possible interactions. I think, however, the examples I have mentioned are

148

sufficient to illustrate that not only do we lack a great deal of knowledge, but the evidence we have so far lends a good deal of credibility to the theory that there is probably a link between genetic and/or chemical-biological events and the condition of transsexualism. Brain function is unquestionably affected by hormones and other chemicals, and it is very possible that when genetic triggers start the process of the development of male or female physiology, the brain, for reasons which are still not clear, may receive quite different signals. Birth defects which cause various forms of hermaphroditism occur in this manner, and a significant amount of evidence points to such a possibility in the case of transsexualism.

Much of the problem with solving the origins of the dilemma of transsexualism lies in the fact that the condition relates to feelings which are virtually impossible to test with verifiable, empirical evidence. Hermaphroditism and many other physical birth defects can be seen, and the evidence is visible to the naked eye, the microscope or can be substantiated with reliable, proven tests. This is not the case with transsexualism, and the tendency is always to deny what we cannot see. Most persons assume transsexuals pursue gender congruity for perverse reasons; in actuality, they are simply proceeding on what their inner feelings tell them about their gender identity. Transsexuals usually do not act upon those feelings until they become adults, and therein lies part of the problem. Adults are supposed to know what gender they belong to and behave accordingly. When transsexuals say they are not what they appear to be, the world looks askance. No moral considerations are presented when little babies, sometimes only weeks old, are operated on for physical birth defects. Medical science gladly comes to their rescue with the support and encouragement of the public. But transsexualism concerns feelings, and understanding our feelings takes many years of living. We cannot operate on babies and small children on the basis of feelings, because only maturity can bring feelings into focus. There is nothing tangible to correct in the case of babies who may in fact be transsexuals. Perhaps research will one day allow us a closer look at the dynamics of the origin of transsexualism, but until that day arrives, transsexualism has to be treated through rehabilitation of adults who have gender discomfort, followed by surgical intervention. Just because transsexuals have to wait until adulthood to correct their problems, however, is no reason to pass judgment on what they say they feel. To do so is inhuman and a manifestation of discrimination in its worst sense. It has not been all that long since science proved there were such things as bacteria and viruses. Until others were shown, through the microscope, that they did indeed exist, most people scoffed at the idea that there were invisible, living organisms all around us and even inside of us and on our bodies. When the microscope demonstrated the reality of their existence, those who doubted reluctantly acknowledged that they had been wrong. We should learn from this example, and not simply condemn something we cannot readily see. When transsexuals are denied the right to pursue gender congruity, they are given life sentences in emotional prisons. Transsexuals are human beings, with all the foibles and strengths which make up the human race. They are men and women who should be judged, not on their conditions, not on their preferences, but on the same basis we evaluate all men and women: Do we enjoy their company? Are they nice? Are they honest? What are their moral standards? Are they considerate? These are the kind of attributes we examine when we meet others. When we apply a different set of standards in judging certain people based on some extraneous factor having little to do with human attributes, we have a very descriptive term for those double standards: it is called prejudice!

In July of 1984, a pair of Siamese twins were separated by surgery. The twins were about nineteen months old at the time. They were joined at the pelvis, had only partial right and left legs respectively, and shared a common liver along with some other internal organs. What makes their story poignant, unusual, and germane to this discussion, is that they shared a single set of external male genitalia. According to news accounts, some discussion took place prior to surgery between the surgeons and the parents regarding the sex of these twins. The reports indicated that the surgeons had offered the parents the alternative of making both of the children females, but the parents had expressed a desire to have at least one boy. One of the twins, therefore, was given an additional "sex change" operation. That baby was surgically provided with a vagina and would, presumably, be raised as a girl. Further accounts indicated that both babies would have to be given hormones in order to bring about normal puberty; so, we would have to speculate that the testes which would have eventually produced testosterone in the male child were absent, not functional, or they could not be preserved through the surgical process.

This is not the first case in medical literature where so called "sex change" operations have been performed on babies. It has been done in some cases of pseudohermaphroditism (i.e., where a baby might have been born with internal female reproductive organs, but some external male genitalia such as a penis). These types of surgeries are not performed routinely by any stretch of the imagination, but when surgery will allow a child to grow into adulthood with compatible sexual organs, reproductive organs, and gender roles, they are considered to be legitimate surgical procedures.

The case of the Siamese twins with shared male genitalia raises some very interesting questions. While little if any fuss has been made over the ethics of the surgery itself, legitimate questions concerning gender roles and transsexualism are at issue here. It would seem that boys or girls must have track records in specific gender roles before eyebrows are raised if decisions are made to have surgical procedures to facilitate living in opposite gender roles.

There simply is no way of knowing how this situation will ultimately develop. Let me play "devil's advocate" for a moment. Suppose the little girl who had the "sex change" operation grows up and, when she is an adult, announces she is a transsexual. Would the psychiatrists who maintain that transsexualism is a psychiatric condition oppose this woman having hormone therapy, counseling, and surgical procedures to help her live in the male role? They would be caught in a dilemma, would they not? Hoist by their own petard, as it were. What has caused this young woman's expressed desire to live in the male role? A psychiatric condition? I should think not! Although she may develop a psychiatric condition due to her situation, can her desire to live in the male role be blamed upon relationships with her mother or her father? Her upbringing? Unlikely! The fact that she was born with a male gender orientation but, because of surgical decisions made by others when she was a baby, she was forced to live in a role she was not comfortable in? Much more likely!

A number of studies appear in the literature concerning babies who, for a number of reasons, have been raised in gender roles different from those they were assigned at birth. One very well known case concerned a male baby whose penis was accidently severed, and a decision was made to surgically remove his testicles, provide him with a vagina, put him on a hormone program designed to coincide with the normal hormone production of a female as she would develop, pass through puberty and into adulthood; the child would then be raised as a female. The experiment was successful, and it is reported that the child eventually adjusted well in the female role as a woman. This particular case has been cited by some to prove that environmental conditioning is the key to gender orientation. Other cases exist in the literature where similar types of situations have resulted in quite different results. The net result is that no one has come up with any conclusive proof as to how children will adjust in gender roles different from those they would normally be assigned to at birth based upon their sexual and reproductive organs. An excellent discussion of this topic appears in Chapter 7 of a recently published book, SEX AND THE BRAIN (Jo Durden-Smith and Diane Desimone, Arbor House, 1983). I can highly recommend this book to anyone interested in exploring this subject in more detail.

No one really knows what will happen to the Siamese twin who is to be raised as a girl, and profound decisions have been made about her role in life based upon assumptions. Firstly, if the baby has reasonably normal appearing female genitalia (although no female reproductive organs) and is raised in the female role, she will be content in that role. This may or may not happen, we just have no conclusive proof that the assumption is correct. Secondly, since one baby was less active than the other, the more active baby should remain the boy. If ever there was a sexist assumption, this has to be it. This type of gender role stereotyping may perpetuate folklore, but where is any significant evidence to demonstrate that boy babies are active and girl babies are passive by nature? That sort of belief is founded upon our social perceptions of acceptable and appropriate male and female behavior springing from anecdotal accounts, not scientific evidence. We want and expect boy babies to be active, girl babies to be cuddly and passive. I ask the readers to weigh their perceptions against the realities. Observe parents, relatives, and friends handling and communicating with small babies. Invariably little boy babies are handled more actively, moved around a lot, and verbal communication is much less frequent than with girls. Girl babies, on the other hand, are more apt to be rocked, cuddled, cooed at and talked to, and generally treated more gently. In point of fact, we start the socialization process of teaching children behavior patterns in gender roles virtually from the day they enter this world.

Certainly no one can fault the decisions of the parents or the physicians involved with the Siamese twins. They made very tough choices with what little knowledge was available to them, and under very difficult circumstances; their decisions must have been agonizing. I only want to stress the reality that no one really knows what will happen; and we must ask: should this baby turn out to be a transsexual, what judgments will be made in the future about any decisions *she* might make as an adult with respect to her gender role? This is exactly why I have challenged rather harshly individuals who feel they have the right to make judgments concerning transsexuals, because their judgments are usually based upon beliefs, assumptions, ignorance, and questionable personal morality. We know *far less* than we have *knowledge of* the processes of life, and anyone who purports to be a scientist and makes judgments based upon theory and ignorance is a charlatan, not a scientist. Science is based on knowledge gained from imagination, theory, speculation, and the testing of facts against all of these by accepted scientific investigation. Preconceived judgments have no place in the scientific world. Legitimate scientists do not set out to prove beliefs. They investigate facts in the hope of proving or disproving theories they have advanced. The difference between these two approaches is similar to the difference between astrology and astronomy. Astrologers use observations of the location of stars and constellations to project personality traits of people based upon their dates of birth, and the location of stars and constellations at that time. Astronomers use knowledge of the structure of the universe to advance theories about such things as the evolution of life, and then test their theories with their observations. The former is show business at best, charlatanism at worst. The latter is science.

Professionals who treat transsexuals do not claim "cure." They only do what their limited resources and knowledge allow them to do: rehabilitate adult transsexuals in opposite gender roles and surgically alter their sexual characteristics to be compatible with those roles, thereby relieving gender discomfort. The very sad case of the Siamese twins I mentioned only serves to illustrate the need for *more knowledge*; not pronouncements served up as a vapid stew, the ingredients of which lack intellectual nutrition and are nothing more than personal beliefs, speculation, and ignorance. Garnishing this mixture with religiosity or loaded studies designed to prove personal theories or beliefs which have no relevance to the relief of gender discomfort adds no substance to this empty concoction and is the height of arrogance.

During the course of my research for this book, I listened as many transsexuals tried to describe to me their relationships with their loved ones, and how difficult it was to get across the frustrations they were struggling with internally. I also talked to many loved ones about their own feelings concerning declared transsexuals that they loved. Although many of these loved ones were trying very hard to accept transsexuals, a large portion of them continued to think of those transsexuals in their biological gender roles. They just could not make the transition from knowing them, first as boys and girls, finally as men and women, and accept them in other gender roles. Many continued to use inappropriate personal pronouns, even long after former transsexuals had completed the gender congruity process. It is totally frustrating when a mother or father calls a former male-to-female transsexual, "him" long after she has been living in the female gender role. This is equally true for female-to-male transsexuals. The personal gender identities of former transsexuals are considerably more fragile than those of most persons. As the years go by, this becomes less of a problem; but, transsexuals in cross living situations, and former transsexuals who have just completed the gender congruity process, are very vulnerable, and their situations are very much like young teenagers who are just beginning to explore their personal gender identities.

Perhaps the biggest roadblock loved ones encounter is one they set up themselves, almost always unintentionally. From what I have been able to observe, most loved ones of transsexuals seem to be reacting to their own feelings, rather than the dilemmas of the transsexuals. Most seemed more concerned about what they may have done wrong, or how friends and others would react and behave toward them, than the effect the dilemmas have had and will continue to have on those they love. In all fairness, many transsexuals become very defensive and only think of their own problems; some give little thought as to how their actions may affect others. Overall, however, I feel that if loved ones were to address their own responses and learn to see them for what they are, they would stand a much better chance of learning to accept transsexuals they love in opposite gender roles. In reality, loved ones are not going to be able to accept transsexuals in other roles unless they do address their own feelings and reactions. Most people find such close examination of themselves quite painful, and the realities of their own motivations, responses, and reactions frequently are glossed over in lieu of meeting them directly. Unless loved ones are willing to undertake some self-examination, acceptance of transsexuals in opposite gender roles will likely be very superficial at best.

It is my hope that readers of this book — friends and loved ones of transsexuals in particular — will have gained a little better understanding of the real dilemma transsexuals are confronted with, perhaps, guided with this understanding, they may be able to address their own reactions and feelings with a little more objectivity. Throughout this book I have used the term "gender discomfort" in reference to transsexuals. This term is, perhaps, somewhat misleading. The word discomfort does not connote unbearable pain, or anything close to it. All of us live with some discomfort from time to time during our lives, and it certainly does not cause us to want to do something as radical as change genders. Gender discomfort, as applied to transsexuals, means a great deal more than mild discomfort. Transsexuals undergo very real, agonizing emotional pain and usually suffer from a relentless drive which often results in compulsive behavior. There seems to be little they can do to control this drive, and the urge for completion dominates their lives. In childhood the compulsion usually takes the form of cross-dressing, and a preoccupation surrounded by confusion and fear. In adulthood it progresses into a desire to translate fantasies, drives, and compulsions in the direction of actually changing their gender roles. The feelings are wrenching, guilt-ridden, and usually terribly disruptive of their lives. So, make no mistake; gender discomfort is something few could tolerate in their lives without trying to resolve it. To be confronted with a loved one who is a declared transsexual is often a devastating blow. I hope the blow can be softened somewhat with some knowledge of what that loved one has had to deal with for so many years of his or her life. Transsexuals often overlook what effect their decisions will have on those who love them. In contrast, many loved ones will condemn transsexuals out of hand and never try to understand their feelings and needs. If this book serves to create some mutual understanding and respect for the feelings of people who love one another, my time will surely have been well spent, and the knowledge that I have helped to create a more favorable climate for mutual understanding would bring me a great deal of personal satisfaction.

**RESEARCH SUPPLEMENT AVAILABLE
FROM THE PUBLISHER**

$14.95

# APPENDIX

The questions which appear on the following pages are the heart of the interviews I conducted with seventy transsexuals. In the research supplement (available separately from the publisher), the interviews are divided into two groups: Male to female transsexuals, and female to male transsexuals. I made this division for two reasons. Firstly, I felt some comparisons between the two groups would prove to be valuable, in some cases, and this was certainly true. Secondly, some of the questions I asked one group would not have been pertinent questions to ask the other group. This is particularly true with respect to the section on medical histories.

The interviews were solicited by me through therapists and physicians who have extensive experience dealing with transsexuals. Each person was paid twenty five dollars for taking part in the interview. I found it quite interesting and revealing that several persons told me I did not need to pay them, and they just wanted to contribute to the book. I did pay them, of course, although two persons refused to accept the money and asked that it be donated to a favorite charity if I insisted on paying; in those cases, this is what I did. I mention this to illustrate that many transsexuals who volunteered to be interviewed seemed to have a genuine concern for a book to be written which presented transsexualism as it is; not how it is conceived by the few individuals who have written autobiographies, or by physicians and therapists who treat transsexuals, or Freudian theorists who tend to view all human conditions as pathological in nature.

The interview was designed, not to psychoanalyze the feelings, emotions, and behavior of transsexuals; rather, it was designed to find out what those feelings, emotions, and behavioral patterns were, and how they had affected those persons' lives. I asked very few questions about sexuality as such. Most of my questions centered around how the persons felt about different matters, including their sexuality. What their sexual fantasies were, I felt, was much more revealing than their sexual practices.

I offered people a choice, and about half of the interviews were conducted at my home; the others asked me to come to their homes. I wanted to make the surroundings as comfortable for them as I could, because I wanted them to open up as much as possible.

Some of the questions in the research supplement were not answered by all the transsexuals in each group. There are two reasons for this: Firstly, a few of the questions I inserted after I had interviewed the first two or three people. Secondly, I tried to keep the interviews on a conversational tone as much as possible. I felt that if the questions were asked in a manner similar to an oral examination, most would not be as responsive as I wanted them to be. It is rather difficult to conduct an interview in this manner and not read the questions word for word. As a consequence, and in all honesty, I simply sometimes overlooked asking a question here and there. I observed this was happening right from the beginning, but I felt it was very important to keep the interviews on as informal a basis as possible. Sometimes when this happened I was able to call the person and fill in the missing answers, but this was not always possible.

The questions and answers in the research supplement make very interesting reading by themselves. I have not relied on statistics, for the most part, however, in writing this book. Rather, I have called on information and insights gained from conducting the interviews. I could not have written the book in the manner in which I have written it simply by using statistics. I combed through all the individual interviews before I started each chapter, and the interviews themselves have provided me with the raw material for this book. I do feel the statistics tell a story in their own right, and they certainly stand on their own merits. My only caution to the reader when reading the questions, and for those who obtain the supplement containing the questions and answers in statistical form, is to remember that transsexualism is a human condition. As such it involves emotions and feelings, and statistics only outline and define the story. They are the skeleton, as it were. The flesh and blood are in the book itself.

# INTERVIEW

## Section No. 1  Family History

1. Did your family live together during your childhood?
2. If yes, are they still together?
3. If separated or divorced, what age were you when that happened?
4. If separated or divorced, which parent did you live with?
5. Did you have an ongoing relationship with the parent who left home?
6. Do you have brothers or sisters?
7. Are your brothers and sisters older or younger?
8. Did any relative live with you when you were a child?
9. Did any other person live with you when you were a child?
10. At about what economic level were your parents?
11. Was there obvious affection between your parents?
12. Were your parents affectionate, warm and loving with you and your brothers and sisters?
13. Was one parent more loving, warm and affectionate?
14. Did your parents favor one child?
15. Did your parents communicate well with you and discuss personal things with you? Such things as feelings, sex, and relationships?
16. What is your present age?

## Section No. 2  History of Relationships

1. Did you, generally speaking, enjoy relationships with other kids as you were growing up?
2. Did you have relationships more with boys or girls?
3. Did you have just casual friends, just a few intimate friends, perhaps a mixture of both, or practically no friends?
4. Did you consider yourself popular, unpopular, or just average?
5. Do you consider yourself shy, outgoing, or a little of both now?
6. Have you ever been extremely introverted and withdrawn?
7. How well did you like and get along with adults as opposed to other kids when you were growing up?
8. How well did you like and get along with your brothers and sisters as a child?
9. How has your relationship with your mother changed since you have become an adult? How does she feel about you concerning your gender discomfort?
10. How has your relationship with your father changed since you have become an adult? How does he feel about you concerning your gender discomfort?
11. How has your relationship with your brothers and sisters changed since you have become an adult? How do they feel about you concerning your gender discomfort?

12. Without giving me a name, who is your best friend? I am interested only in their gender.
13. Generally speaking, are you more comfortable around men or women?
14. In terms of your own sexuality, do you identify more with men or women?
15. Have you ever been married?
16. What is your present marital status?
17. What gender is your spouse or former spouse?
18. Are or have you ever been married in the (female) (male) role?
19. Are you on good terms with your spouse or former spouse?
20. Is or was your relationship a long-term one (5 years or more)?
21. Does your spouse or former spouse support whatever you may decide to do or have done about your gender problem?
22. Do you have any children?
23. If yes, what are their ages?
24. If they are minors, do they live with you, your former spouse, or someone else?
25. Are your children aware of any gender problem you may have?
26. If yes, are they supportive?
27. Does your former spouse encourage your relationship with your children?
28. If your children are minors, do you provide financial support for them?
29. Do you see your children on a regular basis?

Section No. 3 Educational History

1. How far in school did you go?
2. Generally speaking, how were your grades?
3. Did you enjoy school and learning?
4. Have you taken any adult education classes or thought about doing so?
5. Did gender discomfort ever cause you any academic problems at school (i.e.: difficulty in concentrating)?
6. Did gender discomfort ever cause you any social problems related to school (i.e.: difficulty in relating to other kids)?

Section No. 4 Work and Job History

1. What types of work have you performed?
2. Have you ever had a job you liked very much?
3. Have you ever had a job you very much disliked?
4. How do you feel about your present work?
5. Has gender discomfort ever caused you a problem at any job?
6. Have you ever been fired from a job as a result of gender discomfort?

7. Has gender discomfort ever prevented you from getting a job?
8. What are your career goals, both short-term and long-term?
9. Did you shift your gender role in a working situation?
10. If yes, what attitudes did you encounter from your superiors and fellow workers?
11. If you shifted your gender role in a working situation, have you remained at the same job?
12. If you have changed jobs, does anyone at your new place of employment know of your situation?
13. Did you get references from your previous job?
14. Fantasize for me for a minute. This question does not necessarily relate to career. If you could do anything you wanted to and there were nothing to prevent you from doing it, what would you like to do most in life?

Section No. 5 Medical History

1. What major diseases, illnesses, injuries, or surgeries have you had?
2. What was your general health as a child?
3. What is your general health today?
4. If you have any current health problems, please briefly describe them and what medications (including dosage) you may be taking for them.
5. Are you aware of any unusual circumstances or drugs taken when your mother was pregnant with you?
6. If yes, did your mother take D.E.S.?
7. Is there any history of any unusual sexual problems in your family?
8. Is there any history of any serious emotional problems in your family?
9. Does your body function normally in a sexual way (if you take sex hormones, I mean prior to taking them)?
10. Do you consider your genitals normal in size? (Only asked of male to female transsexuals)
11. If no, is this a personal judgment or a medical opinion? (Only asked of male to female transsexuals)?
12. Have you been diagnosed by a physician or a therapist as a candidate for hormone therapy?
13. If yes, was this by a physician or a therapist?
14. Are you under the care of a physician for hormone therapy?
15. If yes, what is the physician's speciality?
16. Has this physician given you a physical?
17. Has this physician ordered blood tests?
18. Have you ever had any psychotherapy?
19. Do you take sex hormones? If yes, what hormones are they and what is the dosage?
20. Do you take any progesterone-like hormones? (Only asked of male to female transsexuals)

21. Have you ever taken sex hormones not prescribed by a physician?
22. If you have taken sex hormones, what effects have they had on you physically?
23. If you have taken sex hormones, what effects have they had on you emotionally?
24. If you are considering shifting your gender role, or have done so, have you had any electrolysis? (Only asked of male to female transsexuals)
25. If yes, how much have you had? (Only asked of male to female transsexuals)
26. How much more do you need to have done? (Only asked of male to female transsexuals)
27. If you are considering shifting your gender role, do you plan to have genital surgery? (Only asked of male to female transsexuals)
28. If yes, where are you considering having the surgery performed? (Only asked of male to female transsexuals)
29. What is the reason you have not had genital surgery to date? (Only asked of male to female transsexuals)
30. If you are considering shifting or have shifted your gender role, do you plan on having or have you had any other surgery to help you make that shift? (Only asked of male to female transsexuals)
31. If yes, what surgeries are you contemplating or have you had performed? (Only asked of male to female transsexuals)
32. Have you had any surgeries to help you shift your gender identity? (Only asked of female to male transsexuals)
33. If yes, what are those surgeries? (Only asked of female to male transsexuals)
34. What is the reason you have not had any or further surgeries to date? (Only asked of female to male transsexuals)
35. Have you ever attempted any genital self-mutilation?
36. If no, have you ever seriously considered it?
37. Have you ever attempted suicide?
38. If no, have you ever seriously considered it?
39. Have you or any member of your family ever had a problem with alcohol or any other drug?
40. If yes, please describe who the person or persons are, what drug or drugs were involved, and a little bit about the surrounding circumstances.

Section No. 6 Transsexual History

1. At what age did you first begin to be aware of any gender discomfort?
2. Did your feelings scare you, confuse you, or please you?
3. Were you aware of your biological gender, though you may have wanted or thought it would be nice to be a (girl) (boy)?
4. Did your feelings of wanting to be a (girl) (boy), and related feelings, intensify at puberty?

5. Did you tell anyone about your feelings?
6. If yes, who was that person and what was their reaction?
7. Did you identify more with boys or girls as you were growing up?
8. Did you play more with boys or girls as you were growing up?
9. Did you enjoy playing more with boys or girls?
10. Were you allowed to play at activities usually associated with (girls) (boys), or did you get scolded or punished if you showed such interests?
11. Did you feel your family felt strongly that you should conform strictly to your gender role?
12. Whom did you identify most with as you were growing up? Your father, your mother, or some other role model?
13. Was your father a masculine man?
14. Was he macho?
15. Was your father a tender and compassionate man?
16. Did your father easily communicate personal feelings?
17. Did he like to participate in family activities?
18. Did he like to play with his children and do things with them?
19. Was your father home a lot?
20. What was your father's occupation?
21. Was your mother a feminine woman?
22. Was your mother tender and compassionate?
23. Did your mother easily communicate personal feelings?
24. Did she like to participate in family activities?
25. Did she like to play with her children and do things with them?
26. Was your mother home a lot?
27. What was your mother's occupation?
28. Did your mother work full-time, part-time, or not at all outside of the home?
29. If either parent was the dominant force in the family, which parent was that?
30. Do you admire your father?
31. Do you like your father?
32. Do you love your father?
33. Do you admire your mother?
34. Do you like your mother?
35. Do you love your mother?
36. How did you first become aware of transsexualism as a condition and relate it to yourself?
37. How old were you when this happened?
38. What was your reaction?
39. If you had sexual fantasies as an adolescent, what gender role did you play in those fantasies?
40. What gender role did any partner play?
41. If you have sexual fantasies now, what gender role do you play in those fantasies?
42. What gender role does any partner play?
43. If you have cross dressed, about when did this begin?

44. How have your cross dressing patterns changed as you have become older?
45. Has cross dressing ever caused you to become sexually aroused?
46. Have you ever had any difficulties with the law because of cross dressing?
47. Has your gender discomfort been a consistent part of your life even if you have tried to repress your feelings?
48. Have you, at times, vowed not to cross dress, etc., and lead a "normal life"?
49. Did you ever think you were (gay) (a lesbian) in your biological gender role?
50. Did you ever explore the (gay) (lesbian) world?
51. Were you not able to relate to others of your gender in your biological gender role?
52. If you decided you were not gay, were you depressed, and did you have the feeling you just did not seem to fit anywhere?
53. From the onset of puberty, which sex has attracted you the most?
54. If you wish to shift your gender role or have done so, what is your sexual preference in that new gender role?
55. Have you had any experience or do you have any way of judging whether you will be able to relate to the persons you want to relate to sexually in that role?
56. Have you had any experience or do you have any way of judging whether persons you want to relate to sexually, if you shift your gender role, will in fact, relate to you?
57. Do you cross live as opposed to cross dressing?
58. Do you envy (women) (men)?
59. Do you admire (women) (men) [as opposed to individual (women) (men) ] ?
60. Do you think of (women) (men) as your sexual peers?
61. How do you feel about your genitals?
62. Do you feel nature somehow short-changed you physically?
63. If yes, are you angry about it?
64. Are or have your sexual fantasies ever been different during masturbation, as opposed to sexual activity with another person, with respect to roles played? (Only asked of male to female transsexuals)
65. Have you ever felt you were really in love?
66. If yes, was it with a man or a woman?
67. Did you have crushes as a teenager?
68. If yes, were they on boys or girls?
69. If you were told transsexualism could be eliminated from your life by psychotherapy, would you seek help?
70. Is there anyone you know for whom you have great admiration?
71. If yes, is this a man or a woman?
72. What fears and concerns do you have or did you have about shifting your gender role?

The following questions were only asked of former transsexuals.

73. When did you have genital surgery?
74. Where did you have genital surgery?
75. Where did you have a hysterectomy and ovarectomy? (Only asked of former female to male transsexuals)
76. When did you have a hysterectomy and ovariectomy? (Only asked of former female to male transsexuals)
77. Where did you have a bilateral mastectomy? (Only asked of former female to male transsexuals)
78. When did you have a bilateral mastectomy? (Only asked of former female to male transsexuals)
79. What physical problems, if any, have you had as a result of the surgery? (Only asked of former male to female transsexuals)
80. Have you had any physical problems as a result of these surgeries? (Only asked of former female to male transsexuals)
81. What emotional problems have you had as a result of the surgery? (Only asked of former male to female transsexuals)
82. What emotional problems have you had as a result of these surgeries? (Only asked of former female to male transsexuals)
83. Have you been able to follow your surgeon's directions regarding dilation? (Only asked of former male to female transsexuals)
84. Have you had a gynecological examination since your genital surgery? (Only asked of former male to female transsexuals)
85. Have you had pap smears since your genital surgery? (Only asked of former male to female transsexuals)
86. Do you still see your regular doctor for periodic checkups?
87. What hormones and what dosage of them are you taking presently? Please contrast that with the amounts you took before surgery.
88. Have you been given open-ended prescriptions for hormones by a surgeon or any other physician?
89. Have you been sexually active since surgery?
90. If yes, have sexual relations been satisfactory and pleasurable?
91. Are you satisfied with the overall effects of the surgery (cosmetically and functionally)?
92. Have you noticed any physical or emotional changes in your behavior or responses to others since the surgery?
93. Have your perceptions of yourself, other people, and the world in general changed at all since your surgery?
94. If you become emotionally involved with a partner, do you intend to tell that person about your transsexual past?

95. Can you tell me a little bit about how shifting your gender role through surgery has affected the overall quality of your life?

Section No. 7  Personal Opinions

1. Putting aside physical appearance, how do you perceive men and women as different in their emotional makeup?
2. Have your responses to situations in life been the way you perceive the opposite gender would respond emotionally, or have they been more typical of your biological gender?
3. Do you feel you are capable of dealing with the physical and emotional aspects of shifting gender roles?
4. Are you aware emotionally as well as intellectually of the finality of gender surgery?
5. How do or will your loved ones ultimately deal with your changes, should you have gender reassignment surgery?
6. Suppose you could not perform sexually in the opposite role. Would you still want to have the surgery?
7. Have you ever been involved in the politics of the gender community?
8. Due to women's liberation and other factors, the roles of men and women have been changing somewhat in our society. These changes seem to be affecting men as well as women and their relationships. Are you comfortable with these changes?
9. Are you ashamed you are a transsexual?
10. Are you proud you are a transsexual?
11. Do you feel the terms "ashamed" and "proud" are not relevant terms?
12. Do you feel life will be easier and more comfortable for you after surgery?
13. Do you feel surgery will solve your emotional problems, other than gender discomfort?
14. Suppose, for a moment, there were no such word as "transsexualism", and no treatment for the condition, surgical or otherwise. How would you deal with the rest of your life?
15. Do you feel you or anyone else could have done anything to avoid your being a transsexual?
16. What have you read on the subject of transsexualism?
17. What do you feel is the cause of transsexualism?
18. What role do you feel therapy, if any, should play for transsexuals?
19. Do you feel there will ever be a preventative or "cure" for transsexualism?
20. Do you feel religion or spiritual involvement can provide personal strength for transsexuals?
21. What factors do you feel should be considered when diagnosing transsexualism?
22. Do you feel surgery should be available on demand?
23. If not, what controls do you feel are necessary?

24. Are you aware of the Standards of Care?
25. If yes, what is your opinion of them?
26. Do you feel most persons who identify as transsexuals are, in fact, transsexuals?
27. Do you feel transsexuals are usually confused about gender?
28. Do you feel transsexualism is in any way related to homosexuality?
29. Do you feel transsexualism is in any way related to transvestism?
30. Please give me a definition of "gender role".
31. Please give me a definition of "gender identity".
32. Please give me a definition of "sexual preference".
33. What are your feelings about women's liberation? Are you supportive of it?
34. Are you satisfied with the services that are presently available to help transsexuals?
35. If no, please tell me what faults you find.
36. What writing, event, news item, or whatever have you seen, read, or heard, if any, that presents transsexualism in a truthful, realistic, and sensitive way, in your opinion?
37. Conversely, what types of things have you seen, read, or heard, if any, that you feel presents transsexualism in an untruthful, unrealistic, and insensitive way?
38. Do you have any ideas that might help to present transsexualism in a truthful, realistic, and sensitive way?

# INDEX

172

# KIM ELIZABETH STUART

Ms. Stuart was born and raised in Oakland, California. She attended local schools and a nearby university. She has four children, all of whom are now adults. Apart from her personal life, she shares the concerns many people have in our fast-paced world. Disability and the attitudes society has with respect to those who are disabled are issues of deep concern to her and a subject she intends to address.

Ms. Stuart has had a life-long concern about the planet we live on and other forms of life that exist here. She sums up her feelings in this manner: ''I am troubled that societies--men and women--have not yet found ways of living at peace with each other. This fact is reflected in the way we view the earth we live on. Instead of trying to live in harmony with nature, we continue to look for ways to force nature to exist by <u>our</u> laws. We take up more than our share of space on this earth, it seems to me, and we are determined, apparently, to allow only those forms of life to exist which serve our needs. We are doing more than biting the hand that feeds us--we are slowly strangling the very thing which gives rise to life and which sustains life. We must look for ways of controlling our predatory nature, or there simply will be no life.''

# METAMORPHOUS PRESS

**Metamorphous Press** is a publisher of books and other media providing resources for personal growth and positive change. MP publishes leading-edge ideas that help people strengthen their unique talents and discover that we are responsible for our own realities. Many of our titles center around Neurolinguistic Programming (NLP). NLP is an exciting, practical, and powerful model of observable patterns of behavior and communication and the processes that underlie them.

**Metamorphous Press** provides selections in many useful subject areas such as communication, health and fitness, education, business and sales, therapy, selections for young persons, and other subjects of general and specific interest. Our products are available in fine bookstores around the world.

Our distributors for North America are:

Baker & Taylor
Bookpeople
Inland Book Co.
Metamorphous
  Advanced Product Services

Moving Books, Inc.
New Leaf
Pacific Pipeline
The Distributors

For those of you overseas, we are distributed by:

Airlift (UK, Western Europe)
Specialist Publications (Australia)

New selections are added regularly and availability and prices change, so ask for a current catalog or to be put on our mailing list. If you have difficulty finding our products in your favorite store, or if you prefer to order by mail, we will be happy to make our books and other products available to you directly. Your involvement and interest in what we do is always welcome. Please write or call us at:

## Metamorphous Press
P.O. Box 10616
Portland, OR 97210
(503) 228-4972

## TOLL FREE ORDERING
## 1-800-937-7771

## Which subjects are you interested in?
### Please check the boxes that apply.

☐ Business/Sales       ☐ Neurolinguistics

☐ Children's Subjects    ☐ Products

☐ Education            ☐ Personal Development

☐ Health/Fitness      ☐ Relationships

☐ Music/Arts         ☐ All of the above

**We'll send you free information on your
areas of interest, as well as
our catalog listing hundreds of books,
tapes, videos and software.**

**YES! Please send a free information packet to** ☐ me
                                                         ☐ a friend

Name_____

Address_____

City _____

State/Zip_____


Name_____

Address_____

City _____

State/Zip_____


Name_____

Address_____

City _____

State/Zip_____


**Mail to:**          **Metamorphous Press**
                               **P.O. Box 10616**
                               **Portland, OR    97210-0616**

**or call toll free:**     **1-800-937-7771**

If you are unable to obtain *The Uninvited Dilemma* at your favorite bookstore, you are welcome to order directly from us by one of the following:

- **Call toll free** with your credit card number
  **1-800-937-7771**

- Mail this form with your credit card number

- Mail this form, including $12.95 check or money order for each copy.
  Add $3.50 for shipping first copy and $0.75 for each additional copy.

VISA _____   MC_____   AMEX _____   OPTIMA _____

Day  Phone     _____

Card Number    _____

Expiration Date  _____

Signature     _____


**BILLING ADDRESS**        Residence  ❐      Commercial  ❐

_____

_____

_____

Orders sent UPS to street addresses (7-10 days), bookrate to P.O. Boxes (2-4 weeks).

| | Quantity | | Total |
|---|---|---|---|
| Uninvited Dilemma | _____ | $12.95 | _____ |
| Research Supplement | _____ | $14.95 | _____ |
| Shipping/Handling | | | _____ |
| **TOTAL** | | | _____ |

**Metamorphous Press**
P.O. Box 10616
Portland, Oregon 97210

If you are unable to obtain *The Uninvited Dilemma* at your favorite bookstore, you are welcome to order directly from us by one of the following:

- **Call toll free** with your credit card number
  **1-800-937-7771**

- Mail this form with your credit card number

- Mail this form, including $12.95 check or money order for each copy.
  Add $3.50 for shipping first copy and $0.75 for each additional copy.

VISA _____     MC_____     AMEX _____     OPTIMA _____

Day Phone _____

Card Number _____

Expiration Date _____

Signature _____

**BILLING ADDRESS**        Residence ❐        Commercial ❐

_____

_____

_____

Orders sent UPS to street addresses (7-10 days), bookrate to P.O. Boxes (2-4 weeks).

| | Quantity | | Total |
|---|---|---|---|
| Uninvited Dilemma | _____ | $12.95 | _____ |
| Research Supplement | _____ | $14.95 | _____ |
| Shipping/Handling | | | _____ |
| **TOTAL** | | | _____ |

- - - - - - - - - - - - - - - - - - - - - - - - - - - - -
Fold here

Place
stamp
here

**Metamorphous Press**
P.O. Box 10616
Portland, Oregon  97210